MW00367001

The ELIXIR *of* IMMORTALITY

The ELIXIR *of* IMMORTALITY

A Modern-Day Alchemist's Discovery of the Philosopher's Stone

ROBERT E. COX

Inner Traditions
Rochester, Vermont • Toronto, Canada

Inner Traditions
One Park Street
Rochester, Vermont 05767
www.InnerTraditions.com

Copyright © 2009 by Robert E. Cox

All rights reserved. No part of this book may be reproduced or utilized in any form or by any means, electronic or mechanical, including photocopying, recording, or by any information storage and retrieval system, without permission in writing from the publisher.

Library of Congress Cataloging-in-Publication Data
Cox, Robert E.
The elixir of immortality : a modern-day alchemist's discovery of the philosopher's stone / Robert E. Cox.
p. cm.
Includes bibliographical references and index.
ISBN 978-1-59477-303-7 (pbk.)
1. Alchemy. I. Title.
QD26.C69 2009
540.1'12—dc22

2009021781

Printed and bound in the United States by Lake Book Manufacturing

10 9 8 7 6 5 4 3 2 1

Text design by Priscilla H. Baker
Text layout by Virginia Scott Bowman

This book was typeset in Garamond Premier Pro with Caxton and Agenda as display typefaces.

To send correspondence to the author of this book, mail a first-class letter to the author c/o Inner Traditions • Bear & Company, One Park Street, Rochester, VT 05767, and we will forward the communication.

Contents

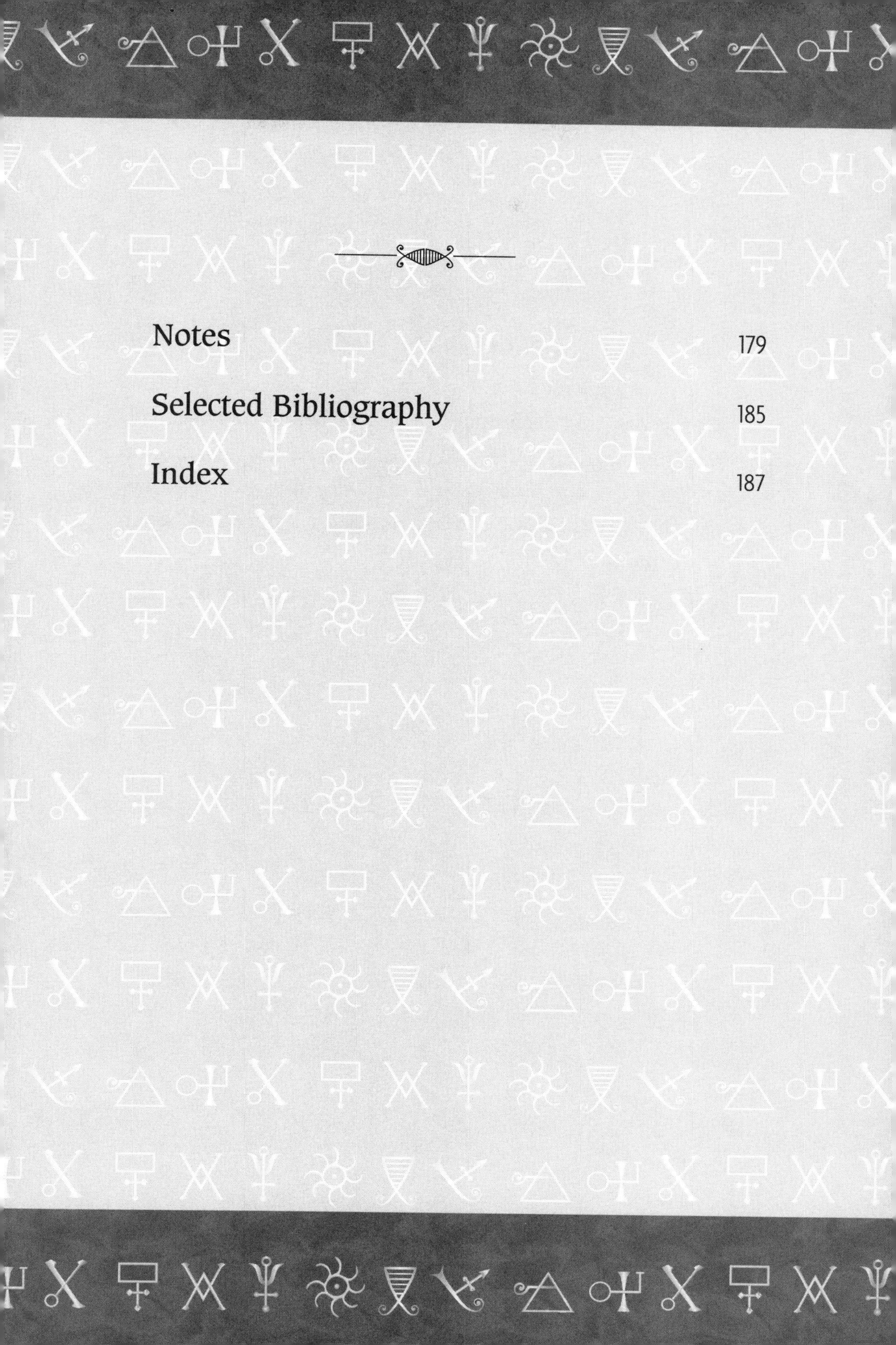

Note to the reader

This book is intended as an informational guide. The remedies, approaches, and techniques described herein are meant to supplement, and not to be a substitute for, professional medical care or treatment. They should not be used to treat a serious ailment without prior consultation with a qualified health care professional.

Preface

In 1989 a series of patents were filed by a wealthy American farmer named David Hudson, who claimed to have discovered a new form of matter. According to his story, which has become somewhat of a folk legend on the Internet, Hudson discovered that his property, consisting of several thousand acres in southern Arizona, contained deposits of gold and the platinum-group elements. Since he already had the earth-moving equipment, Hudson decided that he would attempt to recover some of the precious metals and store them in a safety deposit box as a hedge against inflation and taxes.

But he encountered some serious recovery problems. The deposits were in the form of micro-clusters, small atomic aggregates of the metals, which are notoriously difficult to recover. When Hudson attempted to recover the metals using standard wet chemistry methods, he obtained a white flocculent material resembling dissolved tissue paper, which, when dried, assumed the form of a fine white powder. Mystified as to what this powder might be and why he was not recovering the metals, he sent it out for assay. The assay results showed that it was "nothing."

This seemed pretty strange to Hudson. He reasoned that since he could hold the powder in his hand, it must be something. But none of the standard assay techniques could tell what the material was. It didn't match any of the known chemical elements.

To get to the bottom of the mystery, Hudson hired the best

metallurgical chemist he could find in the Southwest to do research on the material and identify it. After several years of research, costing several million dollars, a method was eventually found to assay it. The methodology was taken from Russian metallurgical scientists, who had been faced with similar problems. It involved a ninety-second carbon-arc fire assay.

A carbon-arc assay is often used to identify elements in a sample of ore. It involves placing two large carbon electrodes in close proximity to each other, between which a small sample of the ore is placed. When a strong electric current is passed between the electrodes, an electric arc is produced with a temperature of approximately 5,000 degrees Celsius. This arc literally vaporizes the ore sample within fifteen seconds, and the vaporized elements can then be assayed by spectroscopic analysis.

Normally, such a burn will vaporize everything, including all of the metals within the sample. But the problem with Hudson's white powder was that it didn't vaporize in a standard fifteen-second carbon-arc burn. As a result, the elements it contained couldn't be identified. Another problem was that if the arc is sustained for longer than fifteen seconds, the carbon electrodes themselves start to break down due to oxidation, which terminates the arc.

The Russians developed a method for sustaining the arc longer than fifteen seconds by conducting the assay in an inert atmosphere, devoid of oxygen, so that the carbon electrodes would not erode by means of oxidation.

When Hudson and his metallurgical chemist performed a ninety-second carbon-arc assay on the mysterious white powder, they discovered that toward the latter stages of the burn, the material began to vaporize and the spectroscopic equipment read off the platinum-group elements and gold in the order of their vaporization temperatures. In other words, the mysterious white powder consisted only of the platinum-group elements and gold—but in a form completely unknown at the time.

Needless to say, this intrigued Hudson, because he had already determined that the ore on his property contained 2,400 ounces per ton of the mysterious white powder! If he could recover it and transform it from the white powder state back to the ordinary metallic state, he would be a rich man indeed. So Hudson retained his metallurgical chemist and asked him to continue research to see if he could determine various means by which the metals could be converted into the white powder state and back to a metallic state.

Eventually Hudson filed patents in the United States, Britain, and Australia on the mysterious white powder, which he and his chemist had determined were monatomic forms of the precious metals, whose electron orbits had been rearranged such that they no longer displayed the physical, chemical, or electrical properties of the original metals. Hudson referred to these materials as "ORME," which is an acronym for orbitally rearranged monatomic elements. The term "monatomic" refers to a single (mono) atom, which is not bound to other atoms by any type of binding mechanism.

Around this time, Hudson's father-in-law approached him with a book about alchemy, which talked about the white powder of gold and its miraculous healing and recuperative powers. Up to that point, Hudson knew little about alchemy, except that it was some medieval theory about being able to transmute base metals into gold. The book described a white powder of gold, produced by alchemical means, that could be ingested for miraculous benefits. Hudson hadn't even thought about eating his white powder, and, being of a conservative nature, was reluctant to do so. He knew for a fact that the white powder was chemically inert, so it couldn't possibly be poisonous, but the idea of eating the metals seemed pretty strange to him.

Being a cautious sort, Hudson took some of the white powder to a local veterinarian and explained his story. They agreed to conduct some experiments on terminally ill dogs, whose bodies were laced with tumors and for whom there was no hope of recovery. Rather than giving the white powder to the dogs orally, they injected it into the animals' bloodstreams in the form of a saline suspension. To their surprise, they found that the dogs miraculously recovered within just a few weeks and were free of tumors.

This caused the wheels in Hudson's mind to start turning. He reasoned that even if he was unable to develop a commercially viable method to transform the white powder into ordinary metals, the white powder itself might be immensely valuable for medicinal purposes and, if the old alchemical texts were correct, possibly spiritual purposes.

He then went on the road and gave a series of lectures around the United States, many of which have been transcribed and are available on the Internet, to raise funds for a large commercial plant to produce the white powder for spiritual purposes. Although he firmly believed in the powder's medicinal value, Hudson was wary of the regulations involved in the medical and pharmaceutical industries and of the problems he might face by making any claims about its "curative" potential. Thus, he touted his white powder as a spiritual panacea, a food for the soul, and compared it to the biblical manna.

Unfortunately, after Hudson raised several million dollars and built his plant, there was an accident in which five thousand gallons of nitric acid leaked from one of the storage tanks at his facility, located outside Phoenix. This sent a plume of poisonous nitrous oxide billowing over a nearby subdivision. More than four hundred people had to be evacuated, and local news stations reported the incident as a major disaster.

Needless to say, the U.S. Environmental Protection Agency shut down Hudson's plant, and required that he move the plant at least ten miles away so it would not threaten any populated area. At that point, Hudson had a series of heart attacks, and his wife threatened to leave him if he continued to pursue his venture. So he gave up on his plant and went back to farming. But the research continued. Although Hudson was no longer directly involved, he continued to hire a chemist to perform the research. During the latter phase of Hudson's work, his main chemist was Don Duke, who actually made the ORME for Hudson and performed research on it. Among other things, Duke determined that ORME are present in volcanic soils all around the world and are naturally absorbed by plants growing in those soils. Duke's research continued with Hudson's blessings.

After several years of research, Duke found that a dozen or so plants and herbs traditionally associated with high nutritional values and healing remedies also tend to accumulate larger quantities of ORME in their leaves, stems, and sap than do other plants. He also found that the brains of higher mammals, such as pigs and cows, tend to accumulate ORME, and can contain as much as 5 percent monatomic elements by weight. This indicated that the elements are associated not only with nutritional and healing plants but also with consciousness.

I myself have been a student of ancient traditions for many years, and in the early 1990s, based upon my own theoretical and metallurgical research, I became interested in alchemy. In the mid-1990s I flew to Phoenix and met with Hudson, and shortly thereafter developed a close and collaborative relationship with his chemist, Don Duke.

In 2002, I was invited by Duke to work with him at his research facility in Utah, and I accepted. Shortly after I arrived and settled into my new home, Duke had a stroke and was unable to continue the work physically, even though his mind remained sharp as a tack. I elected to stay on and continue working in close collaboration with him, so that we might explore the properties of this material further.

So, as fate would have it, I became privy to the secret procedures, somewhat obscured in Hudson's patents, by means of which the naturally occurring ORME are recovered from the ore and pure metals are converted into ORME by wet chemistry methods.

Duke and I both agree that we have barely scratched the surface of a hidden iceberg of enormous potential, which is alluded to in many ancient texts, some of which date back to the very beginnings of human culture and civilization on Earth. The purpose of this book is to share with you my understanding of the ancient science of alchemy and its implications for the future of mankind.

INTRODUCTION

The Ancient Spiritual Science

This is not my first book on ancient traditions and their implications for modern society. In my previous book, titled *Creating the Soul Body,* it was arguably demonstrated that the ancient Vedic, Egyptian, and Hebrew traditions shared a profound spiritual science—literally a science of immortality—which in certain ways rivals and even surpasses our most advanced physical theories. Although I have no intention of repeating the same material in this book, for the sake of our current discussion it is worth reviewing the "scientific" nature of the ancient doctrine.

In essence, the doctrine held in common by the three traditions involved a layered model of the universe. The model was such that the overall organization of the physical universe can be described in terms of underlying metaphysical layers, or layers of consciousness, each of which is tied to its own fundamental space-time scale. The ancients believed that to obtain full immortality in the bosom of the infinite, the soul has to ascend and descend through these layers until it transcends the boundaries of the universe, both above and below. For this reason, the system of layers was compared to a divine ladder, or stairway to the sky, on which the soul could ascend and descend.

This was not just an abstract spiritual doctrine; it was tied to an ancient system of measured arrangement, expressed in terms of matched pairs of space-time scales, which lends itself to empirical evaluation. In *Creating the Soul Body,* I demonstrated that this ancient system could be used to accurately predict a hidden vertical symmetry in the overall organization of the universe.

This symmetry—which links the most fundamental scales of force-matter unification discovered so far on the basis of quantum theory with the most fundamental scales of cosmological organization discovered thus far on the basis of general relativity—is currently unknown in modern theory, but it is nevertheless consistent with the empirical evidence.

The most salient of the matched pairs and their physical correspondences are summarized in the table below, where *L* represents an exponential "layer number."

TABLE OF SIGNIFICANT LAYERS

LAYER NUMBER	10^{-L} CM	MICROSCOPIC	10^{L-1} CM	MACROSCOPIC
L = 12	10^{-12}	Nuclear Unification	10^{-11}	Radius of the Solar Sphere
L = 16	10^{-16}	Electro-Weak Unification	10^{15}	Radius of Heliosphere
L = 24	10^{-24}	Dark-Matter Unification	10^{23}	Radius of Galactic Sphere
L = 29	10^{-29}	Grand Unification	10^{28}	Radius of Hubble Sphere
L = 33	10^{-33}	Super Unification	10^{32}	Radius of Cosmic Egg

This table covers the first thirty-three steps on the stairway to the sky, which take the soul to the "shore of this world," marked by the overall form of the superuniverse, which the ancients compared to a cosmic egg. The ancients went on to map out the stages, steps, or layers of consciousness that deliver the soul to the "shore of the other world," the immortal world of the Supreme Being, which lies beyond the boundaries of the created universe.

In the Vedic, Egyptian, and Hebrew traditions, the path of immortality, which ultimately leads to that "other world," was mapped out as a sequence of forty-two layers, both above and below. In spite of their differences in language, religion, and culture, these three traditions not only counted the same number of layers but also understood them in the same manner.

How and when the three traditions came to have the same knowledge presents a historical mystery of the highest order, which I intend to address in another volume. In this book my focus will be upon the practical aspect of the ancient science that dealt with the material means by which the soul can become immortal.

The ancients all around the Old World shared a belief that certain types of matter, specifically the metals, can be rendered "self-conscious," such that they obtain spiritual qualities. They also claimed to possess simple, low-tech, practical procedures to accomplish this miraculous transformation. This ancient theory and practice, which goes back to the earliest periods of human culture, surfaced in medieval Europe under the appellation "alchemy."

The European alchemists commonly referred to this spiritualized form of the metals as the philosopher's stone, although they admitted it was not really a stone at all but an elixir (powder) produced from the metals. They sought the elixir not so much for spiritual purposes as for monetary ones. Their primary goal was to use the elixir to transmute base metals into gold.

The more ancient traditions, which existed thousands of years prior to the advent of European alchemy, sought the elixir for another purpose. They strove to produce and consume the miraculous substance for the sake of immortality—so that mortality could be transmuted into immortality. For this reason, the ancients referred to it as the food of the gods.

In effect, the ancients viewed the elixir as food for the soul. They claimed that, when consumed, the elixir had the potential to purify the body, mind, and soul so that the initiate would become a fit receptacle for spiritual enlightenment. It was only then that the soul became qualified to ascend the stairway to the sky toward its ultimate goal of obtaining full immortality in the bosom of the infinite. In Creating the Soul Body, the focus was upon theoretical aspect; in this book it will be upon the practical aspect.

The First Practical Sciences

The earliest practical sciences known to man were agriculture, metallurgy, and stone masonry, all of which involved obtaining and fashioning things from the earth. Signs of these three sciences begin to appear during the early Neolithic era, when the first semipermanent settlements, mostly small villages and encampments, begin to show up in the archaeological record.

To support the growing population in these settlements, the ancients developed the science of agriculture, which involved planting seeds in the ground to obtain the fruits, vegetables, and grains needed to feed the people. This was arguably the first popular science, whose secrets were openly shared with the common people so that the growing population could thrive.

The other two sciences were not popular, in the sense that their secrets were not openly shared with the masses. The evidence suggests that those who practiced stone masonry and metallurgy were deemed "craftsmen," and their secrets were passed down through hereditary traditions, often involving initiatory rites.

Moreover, there was a close connection between stone masonry and metallurgy. In order to obtain metals from rocks or stones, one must have a knowledge of stone masonry, or stone cutting. One must know how to cut the stones and thus mine the earth. Once the ores are obtained from the stones, one must then know how to refine the ores in fire to obtain the purified forms of the metals, such as copper, silver, and gold.

A knowledge of masonry was also required to cut stones, or make the earthen bricks, used in the construction of the sacred temples and monuments, which were often adorned with precious metals. In the ancient mind these two processes—the arts of temple-making and metal-making—were intimately linked, and were often performed by the same group of people, who were deemed sacred craftsmen. In the earliest cultures, these sacred craftsmen were part of the priesthood.

Sacred Metallurgy

The oldest-known metals were gold, silver, copper, antimony, iron, lead, and mercury, which were symbolized by the seven planets, or seven divine mountains, and assigned various cosmic and spiritual properties. Although the metals were known by all, the mines from which the metal ores were obtained and the procedures used to refine the ores and produce various alloys were closely guarded secrets.

In ancient Egypt, for example, all of the mines were owned by the royal families and operated under the supervision of the priesthood. Common laborers may have been employed to do the actual mining, but the recovery of metals from the ores and the manipulation of metals to produce various alloys were considered a sacred science, to be conducted only by the priests and their appointed craftsmen, under the condition of sworn secrecy. Commenting on the secret metallurgical practice of the Egyptians, one of the earliest Hellenistic authors on the subject thus stated: "It was the law of the Egyptians that nobody must divulge these things in writing."[1]

The secrecy that surrounded the metallurgical science was reasonable. The discovery of a new metal alloy, from which sharper, harder, or more-durable bladed weapons or agricultural implements could be produced, gave a society a distinct advantage over other societies, and allowed the more knowledgeable society to dominate. For this reason, the ancient metallurgical programs were kept under shrouds of secrecy.

In addition to producing weaponry and agricultural implements, the metallurgical programs were responsible for producing the precious metals, such as gold, silver, and copper, that could be used for trade, for decorating temples, for fabrication of sacred objects, and for displays of wealth. As such, the precious metals added to the secular power of the priesthood and the royal families. In order to secure and maintain their positions of power, the elite ruling classes had to keep strict control over the mining, production, and refinement of metals.

But there was another reason for this secrecy. The ancients believed that certain metals, such as gold, antimony, and mercury, could be used in a secret process to produce a spiritualized form of matter—the elixir of immortality, or food of the gods—which, when ingested, would confer enormous spiritual power. Because the ancient rulers were viewed as embodiments of God on earth, their authority ultimately rested on their spiritual powers.

Toward this end, the priests sought to produce various metallurgical elixirs that would enhance the spiritual power of the ruling classes, so they would remain in tune with the cosmic forces that rule the universe. In medieval Europe, this ancient practice became known as *alchemy,* which was also called the Royal Art because it was used to support the royalty.

The ancient alchemical programs, more than any other, were kept in absolute secrecy, for the alchemical elixirs were the means by which the ruling classes maintained their spiritual authority over the masses and obtained the spiritual insight that served to guide the destiny of the people.

Any mention of such programs in the ancient texts is thus relayed in symbolism and veiled language. It was only when the old societies and kingdoms began to break down that the secret alchemical programs surfaced in public awareness and texts about the secret practices were written. The first alchemical texts thus appeared during the Hellenistic era, when the Ptolemies ruled as the pharaohs of Egypt and ferreted out the secret scrolls of the Egyptian priesthood, putting them on display in the Great Library of Alexandria.

The Great Library

The Greeks had always been jealous of, and somewhat in awe of, the secret wisdom possessed by the Egyptians, whom they viewed as masters of philosophy, architecture, stone masonry, and other disciplines. When the Greeks took charge of Egypt in the third century BCE, they thus made a concerted effort to seek out Egyptian secrets, so that such wisdom might become available to scholars throughout the Hellenistic empire.

Toward this end, the Ptolemies established the Great Library of Alexandria, the first major public library in the world, which in its peak purportedly contained as many as seven hundred thousand ancient scrolls. Scholars from all over the Hellenistic empire, which at that time ranged from Egypt to the borders of India, flocked to the Great Library to study secrets that had been hidden from the eyes of the world since the beginning of time.

It is difficult to imagine the intellectual excitement of those days. For thousands of years Egypt had been the dominant culture in the Western world, and its spiritual and secular power was believed to be rooted in secret knowledge preserved by the Egyptian priesthood. Now, for the first time in history, that secret knowledge was being put on public display with the blessings of the Ptolemies, the Greek-Egyptian pharaohs.

The Ptolemies hoped to revive the secret wisdom of Old Kingdom Egypt, so it could be used to refashion the Hellenistic empire according to the principles that had once made Egypt the greatest nation on earth. Toward this end, they invited Greek, Arabic, and Hebrew scholars from all around the empire to come study the ancient scrolls in an attempt to decipher their hidden meanings.

It was in this milieu that the first alchemical texts began to surface. During this period it appears that a relatively large number of people sought to revive the lost alchemical science, and alchemy was practiced, both successfully and unsuccessfully, over a wide region.

After the fall of the Hellenistic empire and the eventual conquest of Egypt by Rome, the Great Library at Alexandria was destroyed, apparently in a series of fires, and large portions of the ancient port city were swallowed by the Mediterranean Sea.

The Advent of European Alchemy

With the end of the Roman Empire and the subsequent advent of the Roman Catholic Church, the practice of alchemy was largely forgotten or even forbidden in western Europe. Nevertheless, it appears to have survived in Arabic countries and in certain Jewish communities, which were not under the strict authority of the church.

Around the time of the Crusades, alchemical ideas began to trickle back into Europe. The first translation of an Arabic alchemical work into Latin took place in the eleventh century, and soon afterward the medieval tradition of European alchemy began to take shape. Although the church and various European monarchs issued bans against its practice, alchemy flourished throughout Europe in secret societies, who claimed access to a secret knowledge that had been hidden from the eyes of the world since the dawn of time.

It is now recognized that the alchemical practices employed in medieval Europe served as the precursors for modern-day chemistry, metallurgy, and the medical profession, involving the prescription of drugs. Whether or not the European alchemists were successful in producing the fabled elixir, or philosopher's stone, which was the goal of the alchemical practice, is unknown. But their practical methodologies and catalogs of materials paved the way for many modern scientific practices.

The last-known alchemical practitioner of considerable repute was none other than Sir Isaac Newton, who is most famous for laying the scientific groundwork for classical mechanics, or universal laws of motion. But it is now known from Newton's previously unpublished papers that his most ardent passion was the pursuit of alchemy—which involved the quest for the philosopher's stone through the use of gold, mercury, and antimony. It was due to his extensive knowledge of metallurgy that Newton was placed in charge of the British Mint, which made the gold and silver coins that served as the currency of the time.

With the advent of modern chemistry and physics, the practice of alchemy largely died out. The idea that metals can be transformed into a fabulous elixir, capable of rendering the soul immortal and transmuting base metals into gold, is now viewed by most people as a misguided myth.

Origins of the Ancient Practice

The practice of alchemy and the belief in it once pervaded the ancient world, from China to India to Egypt. All around the Old World, the same materials, procedures, and theories were employed in pursuit of the same goal.

The widespread practice of alchemy throughout the Old World is difficult to explain in the context of current theories of cultural dissemination. According to myths and legends surrounding the practice, it was originally received from "divine men," "descended angels," or the "gods," who walked the earth in the predawn history of the human race.

For example, a legend that was already old in China in the third century AD claims that the knowledge of the elixirs was originally received from a divine man:

> A long time ago, while Zuo Yuanfang (Zuo Zi) was devoting himself to the practices of the purification of thought (*jingsi*) on mount Tianzhu (that is, the Taishan mountain, in modern Shandong), a

> Divine Man transmitted to him the Books of the Immortals on the Golden Elixirs.[2]

Similarly, one of the earliest authors on Western alchemy, a Hellenistic writer named Zosimos of Panopolis, refers to a secret Egyptian book of wisdom called *kmy.t* (*kemi*), which encodes secret alchemical formulas that originated with the descended angels—that is, the Egyptian gods.[3] In India, an entire book (the ninth mandala) of the *Rig Veda* is devoted almost exclusively to the elixir (called *soma*) and the means of its production and purification. As in the other traditions, the knowledge of soma was attributed to divine sources.

The Food and Drink of the Gods

The *Rig Veda,* composed in an archaic form of Sanskrit, is currently recognized as the oldest example of Indo-European language ever found on earth. When this and other texts like it were discovered by Western scholars in the eighteenth century, they found that the Sanskrit language of India is intimately linked with virtually all of the ancient and modern European languages. This initiated the study of language groups in general, and the study of the Indo-European language group in particular.

Although the actual composition date of the *Rig Veda* is unknown, it is believed to be at least 3,500 years old and possibly as old as 6,000 years. The Vedic hymns are thus exceedingly ancient, and have not only linguistic importance but mythological, religious, and cultural importance as well.

When scholars began to study the *Rig Veda* and its associated texts, they found that it describes myths, legends, and religious practices that tend to shed light on the myths, legends, and religious practices of all the European countries prior to the advent of Christianity. Commenting on this unique feature, one early Western scholar said:

> As in its original language we see the roots and shoots of the languages of Greek and Latin, of Kelt, Teuton and Slavonian, so the deities, the myths, and the religious beliefs and practices of the Veda throw a flood of light upon the religions of all European countries before the introduction of Christianity. As the science of comparative philology could hardly have existed without the study of Sanskrit, so the comparative history of the religions of the world would have been impossible without the study of the Veda.

In this regard, one of the persistent subjects that pervades the *Rig Veda* and its ancillary texts, and to which an entire book (*mandala*) of the *Rig Veda* is devoted, pertains to a mysterious elixir, variously called *soma* or *rasa,* which was considered the food and drink of the gods.

> Soma is king. Soma is the food of the gods. The gods eat soma.[4]

The Vedic seers (*rishis*) who composed the *Rig Veda* claimed that they had received the knowledge of how to make soma from the gods. The seers ate or drank the soma to find the gods, become enlightened, and attain spiritual immortality.

> I have tasted, as one who knows its secret, the honeyed (soma) drink that inspires and grants freedom, the drink that all, both gods and mortals, seek to obtain, calling it rasa. We have drunk the soma, we have become immortal; we have gone to the light; we have found the gods.[5]

We will examine the nature of soma in more detail later. The point that I wish to make here is that the Vedic seers claimed to possess a mysterious elixir, which could be eaten in a dry form as a "food" or consumed in a liquid form as a "drink," which was ascribed miraculous powers.

The word *elixir* is derived from the Arabic *al* = ("the") and *ixir* ("powder"). As noted earlier, the European alchemists claimed that their fabulous philosopher's stone was not a stone at all, but rather a powder or elixir obtained from the metals to which were ascribed similar miraculous powers. In addition to being able to transmute base metals into gold, the European alchemists claimed that the elixir could be consumed in a dry form as food or suspended in a liquid, such as alcohol or water, and consumed in a wet form as a drink.

The European alchemists, however, had no knowledge whatsoever of the Vedic texts, which were discovered by European scholars only in the late eighteenth century, after the European tradition of alchemy had largely died out. The alchemists of medieval Europe attributed their knowledge to Jewish, Hermetic, Arabic, and Egyptian sources, and not Vedic sources. Nevertheless, as we shall soon see, their practices, materials, and theories were very similar to those described in the Vedic texts, as well as to those described in ancient Chinese texts.

My contention, which I will support with ample evidence, is that ancient cultures all around the world once employed similar practices, materials, and theories in the pursuit of the same goal—to produce a wondrous elixir, made from the metals, to which was ascribed the potential to transmute one atomic element into another, and also to transmute mortality into immortality.

Modern Implications

What are we to make of this ancient practice? Were the ancients laboring under a collective delusion that spanned continents and millennia, or did they actually possess a secret knowledge regarding the material elements, by means of which they were able to create a spiritualized form of matter with miraculous properties?

As discussed in some depth in *Creating the Soul Body,* the ancients clearly possessed a genuine science of consciousness—literally a field theory of consciousness, which may have many important implications for our current pursuit of a unified field theory.

It was not just a science of consciousness, however, but a science of matter as well, and of the relationship between the two. According to the ancients, all forms of matter are but congealed forms of consciousness, produced by a process that they compared to churning milk to produce curds and whey. They held that everything in the material universe is alive, because all things, down to the smallest parts or particles of creation, are endowed with the property of consciousness.

Under ordinary circumstances, however, the particles of matter out of which the material universe is made appear to be insentient, or devoid of consciousness. The ancients compared this to a veil of ignorance, which must be pierced to allow the light of consciousness to shine through. In Vedic or Indian alchemy, this was called piercing (*vedha*).

When the elements become pierced, they cease to behave like insentient forms of matter. Rather, they tend to behave like sentient or spiritualized forms of matter, which act as a source of consciousness and intelligence. By consuming these spiritualized forms of matter, the ancients believed that the bodily intelligence was enhanced, such that the health and longevity of the body was improved. But at the same time, they believed the spiritual consciousness of the soul was enhanced, such that it developed the potential to expand throughout the universe, into the fathomless bosom of infinity.

They also believed that when these spiritualized elements are introduced into a system of unspiritualized elements, they have the potential to liberate the other elements from the binding forces that uphold the identity of those elements, and which keep one element from being transmuted into another. More specifically, the spiritualized elements were viewed as having the potential to catalyze the transmutation of one type of metal into another when the metals are in a molten state.

Even more important, they believed that all of these things could be accomplished using a simple, low-tech, low-energy process, which they kept as their secret of secrets, passed down from time immemorial. The simplicity of the process was also noted by European alchemists, who claimed that once the secret was known, the whole thing became "like child's play and women's work"—that is, as easy as baking a cake by following a recipe. As Philalethes put it:

> I assure you, upon the word of an honest Man, that if this one Secret were but openly discovered, Fools themselves would deride the Art; for that being known, nothing remains, but the work of Women and the play of Children, and that is Decoction [slow digestion under heat]. So that not without cause did the Wise men hide this Secret with all their might.[6]

Although it is healthy to maintain a certain degree of skepticism, let's entertain some "what ifs?". What if the ancients were telling the truth? What if they actually possessed a secret art to produce a completely unknown form of matter, unlike anything that exists on the face of the earth, that has the potential to transmute one atom into another and to render the body healthy and the mind enlightened? If such a process exists, and were rediscovered and made public, then the implications for mankind, both now and in the future, would be inestimable.

Although we may pride ourselves on our modern material science, the fact is that we do not yet possess a science of consciousness, nor do we understand very clearly the relationship between matter and consciousness. Although we now have the ability to transmute one atomic element into another by means of high-energy nuclear reactions, the procedure is very high-tech and involves enormous energy and expenditure. Even if we ignore the health and spiritual claims associated with the elixir, its rediscovery could have enormous implications for material technology and would change the face of modern society.

Are we so arrogant and prideful of our modern accomplishments that we are willing to ignore and cast aside the possibility that the ancients knew something that we do not? Doesn't it make sense that we should at least explore the possibility in more depth? That is precisely the purpose of this book.

My Perspective

This book will not be written from a disinterested academic point of view. It will be written from the perspective of a practicing alchemist, namely myself, who has a passionate belief in the validity of the ancient claims, and has been actively engaged in research to either prove or disprove them, once and for all.

As will be discussed in more detail later, it is my opinion that the ORME (white powder of the metals) discovered by David Hudson is not the real elixir. It is but a precursor of the elixir, a starting material that can be naturally produced within the earth and spewed out in volcanic eruptions. The ancients referred to this type of powder as the "salt of the earth," due to its resemblance to salt—a white powder. But that was only one of its designations. It was also called the white sulfur, the white gold, the manna.

The ORME may very well have some healing and spiritual properties, but it is not the miraculous elixir described by the ancients. That is something else entirely, which is nevertheless related to the ORME—in the same way that a tree is related to its seed. For this reason, the ancients often compared the grains of white powder, obtained from the ores, to the "seeds of the metals."

The focus in this book will not be upon the ORME but upon the production, properties, and applications of the elixir itself, as gleaned from ancient alchemical, religious, and mythological texts taken from around the world.

No doubt we all see the world through our own colored glasses—and I am not immune to this. When I read the ancient literature, I see alchemy implied in almost every page. Whether this is a fault or an insight, I leave to the reader's evaluation.

Alchemical Code Language

The fact is that the science of alchemy was an extremely secret science, and the alchemical authors, both ancient and modern, tended to hide their true meanings under thick veils of symbolism in which the words are not to be taken for their literal meanings.

Even in medieval Europe, the open sharing of alchemical secrets was considered anathema and sure to bring the curse of God. Although the alchemists longed to share their secret with the common man, they felt that the time was not quite right to do so. Thus they wrote their treatises in such a manner that only those deemed worthy of receiving the knowledge, by the blessing of God, would be able to decipher them.

> All Sons of Art . . . write and teach according to that permission which the Creator of all things hath given them . . . And truly it is not our intent to make the Art common to all kind of men, we write to the deserving only; intending our Books to be but as Way-marks to such as shall travel in these paths of Nature, and we do what we may to shut out the unworthy: Yet so plainly we write, that as many as God hath appointed to this Mastery shall certainly understand us, and have cause to be thankful unto us for our faithfulness herein. . . . we hint the way; prayer to God and patient persisting in the use of means, must open these Doors.[7]

To decipher the alchemical secrets, two things are needed: practical experience in working with the metals and minerals and intuitive insight to see through the veils of symbolism associated with the practice. Although I make no claim to be an enlightened seer, I have in the past spent nine years in silent meditation, with my eyes closed, for eight to ten hours a day, and daresay that I have a decent intuition. Moreover, I have spent years working with the minerals and metals in a hands-on manner. So when I read the alchemical, religious, and mythological texts I tend to see things that perhaps others don't.

Although the ancients forbade the alchemical secrets to be disclosed to the public, I have a different perspective, born of our modern times: I believe these secrets are destined to become the province of the common man, and in this book we will attempt to discover them. We are on a quest to rediscover the fabled philosopher's stone.

The Age of Aquarius

The ancients believed that the evolution of the stars in the heavens, as well as the evolution of human culture on earth, is governed by the will of God, which operates nonlocally and is manifested by the influence of consciousness on all things in creation.

They also believed that the nonlocal operation of divine will is such that all things in the universe are tied together into a single harmonious whole. On the basis of this understanding, they developed long-term predictive theories, which tie the evolution of human culture on earth to celestial cycles in the heavens.

Although a detailed analysis of these predictive theories lies beyond the scope of this book, of particular importance is the fact that we are currently on the cusp of the Aquarian Age, marked by the sun's transit through the sign of Aquarius on the morning of the vernal equinox each year.

The ancients assigned symbols to the thirty-degree arcs in the sky through which the sun transits in this manner, such that the symbols were viewed as "signs" of things that have been and things to come. In the Greek tradition of astrology, the sign of Aquarius was represented by a man carrying a pot.

But this is no ordinary man and no ordinary pot. The man is Aquarius, the water-bearer of the gods, and the pot is supposed to contain the drink of the gods, by which the gods become immortal.

In the system of Vedic astrology, called Jyotish, the sign of Aquarius is called Khumba, the pot. According to Vedic mythology, this is the pot carried by Lord Dhanvantari, the patron deity of the Vedic healing science, who appeared at the end of the cosmic churning process carrying a pot of nectar. But again this was no ordinary nectar. It was the nectar of immortality, *amrita rasa,* the drinking of which rendered the soul immortal.

The Sanskrit term *rasa* not only means "nectar," but it also means "blood." The term *amrita rasa* can thus also be translated as "immortal blood," or "holy blood." In this case, the sacred alchemical pot that contains the nectar may be viewed as the Holy Grail (*san gréal*), which contains the holy blood (*sang réal*). This provides but one example of how the Vedic myths tend to shed light on western European myths, such as the myth of the Holy Grail.

At this particular moment in human history, the "sign" of the times is such that the rediscovery of alchemical secrets is favored and imminent. In Vedic astrology, Aquarius is not only the sign of all those who work with metals in the fire but also the sign of the common man.

The implication is that unlike the past, when the science of alchemy was kept hidden and secret as the province of the elite classes alone, in the coming age this science is destined to become public—it will become the province of the common man. In other words, the time longed for by the ancients, when their secrets could be openly shared with the public in accordance with the will of God, is close upon us. In fact, I believe it is here.

Lest there be some confusion, let me state in clear and no uncertain terms that I myself do not yet possess the elixir. Nevertheless, I am on a passionate quest to obtain it. It is hoped that by sharing the knowledge contained in this book, others will be inspired to join in this quest, either collaboratively or independently, for the benefit of all mankind. In my opinion, the time has finally come for the Holy Grail and its mysterious contents to be delivered to us all. May the delivery be swift, for God knows we need it.

ONE

The Art and Science of Alchemy

The Origin of the Word *Alchemy*

The term *alchemy* is commonly attributed to a secret tradition in medieval Europe. But it is now known that similar alchemical traditions of unknown antiquity existed all over the ancient world, extending from China through India and Persia all the way to ancient Middle East and Egypt.

Remarkably, all of these alchemical traditions were based upon similar theoretical principles and used similar materials and procedures in their pursuit of the same goal—to produce a mysterious sacred elixir, to which were ascribed miraculous powers. But these more ancient traditions did not specifically refer to themselves as alchemical traditions and, unlike their European imitators, their primary focus was not the transmutation of base metals into gold, but the attainment of extraordinary spiritual powers and spiritual immortality.

The term *alchemy* is a relatively recent one, whose precise derivation is unknown. But the prefix *al* indicates that the term is Arabic in origin. There are five basic theories concerning the derivation.

The first theory is that the term was derived from the name of ancient Egypt, Km.t (or Khem), which means "black earth." In Arabic this becomes *al-khem,* and hence *alchemy,* meaning the ancient "Egyptian art," or the "art of black earth."

The second derivation comes from the Greek word *chemeia,* which denotes the art of making metal. The third derivation is from the Greek word *chumeia,* which denotes the art of extracting juices or infusions from plants, and thus herbal medicines and tinctures.

The fourth is related to the word *bdellium* (Hebrew *bdolach*) used in the book of Genesis. Although this word means "gum resin," it actually has an alchemical connotation when traced back to its Egyptian meaning. The English word *gum* derives from the vulgar Latin *gummi,* which is a loan word from the Greek *kommi* (for example, see Herodotus II, 86, 96). The Greek word in turn is derived from the ancient Egyptian word *qmy.t* (*qemi* = "gum, resin"). The idea that alchemy is related to various gums is made clear in a number of alchemical texts, that talk about "our gum" as the key to the work.

The fifth derivation comes from one of the earliest authors on Western alchemy, a Hellenistic writer named Zosimos of Panopolis, who refers to a famous Egyptian book of wisdom called *kmy.t* (*kemi*), which encodes secret alchemical formulas that originated with the fallen or descended angels.[1]

The truth is that no one really knows the actual derivation of the word. It should be emphasized, however, that the word only begins to appear in European texts of the medieval era. Prior to that, the alchemical science remained virtually nameless, or was given different names by different traditions, according to the language and culture in which it was practiced.

The Ores

According to the mainstream tradition of European alchemy, there were at least three principal ingredients or raw materials required for the work. They correspond to (1) gold, which was obtained from gold ore, gold dust, or gold nuggets; (2) antimony, which was obtained from a blackish mineral called stibnite (antimony sulfide), and (3) mercury, which was obtained from a reddish mineral called cinnabar (mercury sulfide). All three of these minerals or metals were known in ancient times.

Pure gold was probably the first metal known to man, because it can be found in nature in the form of gold nuggets or gold dust in running streams. As such, it was likely known even in very remote prehistoric times. Quartzite gold would also have been known and probably prized due to the golden or yellow color of the mineral.

Stibnite, or antimony sulfide, was also known and used by very early cultures. When crushed into a black powder, stibnite was used for cosmetic purposes as a form of eye shadow, or for medicinal purposes as a treatment for eye diseases. This was true in the early Vedic, Hebrew, Egyptian, and Persian cultures alike. In the Arabic alchemical tradition, stibnite was called *kohl*—the spirit.

The antimony metal obtained from it was believed to have the potential to infuse the spirit of life into gold, such that the finely divided seeds of gold became alive and thus capable of germinating into the elixir, like the seeds of a plant. With the advent of fermented liquors produced from the seeds or grains of plants, these liquors became known as alcohol, or spirits. More specifically, the spirituous liquors were viewed as containing "the spirit"—*al* + *kohl*—of plants. Molten antimony (kohl), on the other hand, was viewed as containing the spirit of metals.

Cinnabar (or mercury sulfide) was also known and used in very ancient times. The modern word *cinnabar* is believed to come from the Persian word *zinjifrah,* which means "dragon's blood," which in turn is believed to be a corruption of the Sanskrit word for both red lead and cinnabar—*sindura.*

When crushed into a fine red powder, cinnabar was used in ancient times as a red pigment now known as vermillion, or China red. There is evidence that this crushed-cinnabar pigment has been used in both

China and India since prehistoric times. In ancient India this pigment was often used to mark the spot between the eyebrows, the spiritual third eye, with a red dot, called the *tilak,* a practice common in India even today. In modern times, however, red vegetable dyes are used instead of crushed cinnabar.

In the West, the earliest known use of cinnabar has been found at Catyl Hoyuk, one of the world's first cities, located in central Anatolia (Turkey). The ancient city is dated to around 6000 BCE, and is estimated to have had a population of between four thousand and six thousand in its heyday. The pigment from crushed cinnabar was used to paint the skulls of the dead there, apparently for religious or spiritual purposes.

Metals from Ores

Unlike gold, which can be found in a pure metallic state in nature, antimony and mercury typically occur in the form of the sulfide minerals stibnite and cinnabar. Although small quantities of both metals can occur in a pure, or free, state in nature, they are relatively rare. To use mercury and antimony in their alchemical practices, the ancients had to obtain the metals from their ores.

The process of recovering mercury is relatively simple. The cinnabar merely has to be crushed and heated, at which point the mercury becomes released from the sulfur and can undergo a downward distillation to be collected as liquid mercury below. Since the temperatures are not that high, this would have been a relatively easy, low-tech, low-energy process that could have been performed even in Neolithic times using a fire produced from wood.

Recovering antimony is not so simple, however, and the European alchemists made a big deal about the secret process used to produce pure antimony metal from its mineral ore. They claimed that this would serve as a major stumbling block to those who did not know the secrets of the ancients, implying that the process was part of the secret lore that had been passed down since time immemorial. This was one of the "big secrets" of alchemy, often alluded to in veiled and symbolic terms.

Philalethes, an anonymous alchemist said to have come from a well-to-do family, ostensibly in Britain, claimed that he was the first alchemist in the history of the world to speak more or less plainly about this secret process. It is now known that the process described by Philalethes, and referred to by alchemists as the Star Regulus, is relatively simple. In fact, this process is still in use today to recover antimony metal from stibnite.

The process requires a good hot fire, but not exceedingly hot. One could provide the proper fire by making a crude fireplace from bricks or stones and filling it with wooden logs, which are set on fire and the hot coals fanned. Then, when the fire is right, one must throw the crushed stibnite into it. Unlike mercury sulfide, whose chemical bonds can easily be broken by the mere application of heat, the bonds that hold the antimony and sulfur atoms together cannot. A catalyst is required. That catalyst is provided by iron.

When metallic iron, in some form or another, is cast into the fire along with the stibnite, the iron reacts with the sulfur, forming iron sulfide. The iron sulfide sublimes off as a smelly white smoke, leaving behind molten antimony, which dribbles down to the bottom of the fireplace. Upon cooling, the molten antimony will form a brittle blob of metal, which, if pure, will display a crystalline fractionalization pattern on its surface that resembles a star: hence, the term "Star Regulus."

All of this is now clearly understood. The problem is that the archaeological evidence suggests that the procedure for smelting metallic iron was not discovered until the advent of the Iron Age. Other than a single iron rod, found recently in the Great Pyramid and presumably made from meteoric iron, no iron artifacts have been found anywhere in the world prior to 1600 BCE. Before 1200 BCE, such iron objects were extremely rare and valued more highly than gold. Sometime between 1200 BCE and 1000 BCE, the Iron Age actually began, when the process for smelting and fashioning objects from iron became relatively widespread.

On the surface this seems to imply that alchemy, as taught and practiced by the European alchemists, could not possibly have existed prior to around 1200 BCE, which marks the early phase of the Iron Age. This is because metallic iron is required to recover metallic antimony, and metallic antimony is required to produce the seeds of gold, which in turn are used to make the elixir. Without iron, no antimony and no elixir. On the surface, this would seem to contradict our premise that the art and science of alchemy has been practiced since the earliest phases of human civilization. But there may be a way around this difficulty, as discussed in the next section.

The Worthless Refuse of the Slag Heap

The European alchemists commonly made references to a mysterious material used in their work, which was exceedingly cheap to obtain, and which was viewed by many as worthless, something to be thrown away. The pervasive references to this material, in different schools of alchemy, suggest that it was part of an age-old tradition, the knowledge of which had somehow been passed down to them. This material too was viewed as a key to the work—and in particular as a key to the performance of the Star Regulus.

In medieval Europe, ordinary metallic iron was abundantly available for anyone who had knowledge of Star Regulus and wanted to perform it. But at that time, the stoichiometric laws of chemistry had not been developed. The early medieval alchemists didn't know that the stinky white smoke emitted during the Star Regulus consisted of particles of iron sulfide. Moreover, they didn't use iron purchased from a blacksmith to perform the Star Regulus. Rather, they used another mysterious substance, which was inexpensive and readily available, in accordance with the age-old tradition.

The mysterious substance required to perform the Star Regulus was identified with the Roman god Mars, the god of war, often symbolized by the iron weapons of war. So apparently they knew it was a form of iron. But it was not the type of iron one would ordinarily purchase from a blacksmith. It was a very cheap form of metallic iron, which was generally thrown away in ancient times as worthless. To get at the heart of this mystery, we need to consider how iron is smelted.

The earliest-known form of iron ore in the world is *hematite,* a form of iron oxide, which was highly prized and mined by prehistoric cultures around the world. Tens of thousands of years ago, our ancient ancestors all around the world were mining this mineral, crushing it, and using it as a pigment called *ocher* to paint murals on the walls of their caves and to paint the bodies of their dead. Ancient hematite mines are in fact the earliest-known mines on earth.

Of course our prehistoric ancestors didn't know that ocher, or hematite, was actually a form of iron oxide. They just liked it because it could be crushed to make a colorful pigment—the first pigment known to man.

It turns out that metallic iron can easily be smelted from hematite by heating crushed hematite with charcoal, or the ashes from any common wood fire. In the process, the oxygen atoms in the hematite become bonded with the carbon atoms in the charcoal. This produces carbon dioxide, which then boils off as a gas, leaving behind a solid form of pure iron. Because the iron does not need to melt, this can be accomplished at relatively low temperatures, below the melting temperature of iron.

In principle, the ancients—even our prehistoric ancestors—could have produced metallic iron, using nothing more than hematite, charcoal, and a wood fire. The same thing could have been done with siderite (iron carbonate), commonly found along with malachite (copper carbonate) and other copper-bearing ores. In fact, the early copper smelting operations, dating back to at least 5000 BCE, produced this type of metallic iron in abundance. It was produced as a by-product of the copper smelting process. But the ancients did not recognize it as iron.

Whereas the temperatures produced by a primitive furnace or fireplace are sufficient to melt copper, they are not sufficient to melt iron. When copper is recovered from the smelting process it is recovered as a molten metal, which can easily be collected and purified. The metallic iron produced by the same reduction remains solid. It forms what is called the "bloom"—a porous mass of metallic iron mixed with other silicate minerals (the slag), which forms a brittle, hardened mass when it cools.

To make "wrought iron" from the bloom it must be hammered with great force while extremely hot, so that the molten slag squirts out from the porous mass of solid iron, leaving behind more or less pure metallic iron that can then be hammered into a blade or any other wrought-iron object.

But hammering the hot bloom while the slag within it is still molten is an extremely dangerous and difficult process, which was only invented and mastered with the advent of the Iron Age, around 1200 BCE. Prior to that time, the bloom, which was inevitably produced in copper smelting operations throughout the Old World, was simply thrown away as worthless. More than likely the ancients didn't realize that the bloom contained iron in the first place due to the brittle nature of the mass, which doesn't resemble a metal at all.

The idea of hammering the hot bloom to produce wrought iron is not very intuitive. Nor is it something that a coppersmith would naturally want to do, because when hammered with force, the molten slag spews out everywhere, and the coppersmith would have been burned severely when he first tried it. How this process was actually discovered thus remains a mystery, but its discovery initiated the Iron Age, when wrought-iron blades, plow heads, and other utensils began to be made and used on a widespread basis.

But apparently the ancient alchemists discovered that the bloom, the otherwise seemingly worthless material produced as a by-product in the ancient copper smelting operations, or produced directly by simply heating crushed hematite (ocher) with charcoal, could be used to reduce stibnite to pure antimony metal in the secret process that became known as the Star Regulus.

The indisputable fact is that the ancients had access to metallic iron long before the advent of the Iron Age. The ancient copper smelting operations, dating back to 5000 BCE, were sitting on mountainous heaps of slag that they had produced over the years, and that slag was filled with metallic iron.

In those days, iron (mostly obtained from meteors) was much more valuable than gold. If the coppersmiths of the time had actually realized that they were sitting on mountains of metallic iron, they would have had a cow, so to speak. But they didn't. The slag containing the iron was simply thrown away as worthless, and anyone who wanted to carry it away was welcome to do so.

Prior to the Iron Age, the metalsmiths didn't know how to transform slag or bloom into wrought iron. But apparently the alchemical priests somehow realized, or perhaps received the information from their ancient tradition, that this innocuous material had an extremely valuable use in their secret alchemical process.

In effect, the ancient alchemists used the crushed bloom, filled with metallic iron, as the required catalyst in the reduction of stibnite to pure antimony metal. They may not have known that the iron in the material acted as a "chemical catalyst," but apparently they knew that it was a required ingredient in the secret recipe that had been passed down to them since time immemorial.

The understanding presented above completely removes any barrier of time with respect to the development of the art and science of alchemy. All three metals (gold, antimony, and mercury) could, at least in principle, have been produced ten thousand years ago by clever sages, because the ancients knew about all the materials and had all the practical means to do so.

This does not mean that one should expect to find large alchemical sites in the archaeological record. As will be discussed in more detail later, the alchemists typically worked with very small quantities of the three metals to produce the elixir—in fact, the European alchemists recommended that the final production should involve no more than one or two ounces of the metals. Such small operations, carried out by an elite few, would be invisible in the archaeological record.

Philosophic Gold

As noted above, metallic gold was readily available in the form of nuggets and gold dust obtained from streams. In ancient times, gold dust was often gathered from running streams using woolen fleece—or sheep skins. The gold dust would stick to the fleece while the other lighter materials were washed away. This practice provided the basis for the myth of the Golden Fleece, which was linked with the quest for immortality. It was also described in the *Rig Veda,* which tells us that woolen filters were used in the production of soma.

But the gold nuggets or gold dust obtained from nature were not used in their native form. They had to be specially prepared using antimony. This specially prepared form of gold was called philosophic gold. Because this unique and mysterious form of gold was known only to alchemists, they commonly called it "our gold." The preparation of philosophic gold is the key that opens the door to the shut palace of the king (gold), a metaphor used by Philalethes in what many consider his greatest work, called "An Open Entrance to the Shut Palace of the King."

Although there are many alchemical texts and treatises that describe the use of ordinary yellow gold for the work, according to Philalethes these texts were written either by pretenders to the work or by wise philosophers to deceive the unwary. Certainly, the alchemists started with yellow gold, such as that obtained from mines or from gold nuggets, but they then transformed it into something else that doesn't resemble yellow gold at all. This mysterious form of gold was also called the "seed of gold" because it was viewed as being infused with the spirit of life.

Although Philalethes himself described two ways of performing the work, one with yellow gold and one with "our gold," he later confides that the only way to succeed with the work is to use "our gold." He tells us that whatever he has written to the contrary was written only to deceive the unwary.

> But this I know, and can testify, that there is but one way, and but only one Regimen, no more colors than ours; and what we say or write otherwise, is but to deceive the unwary: For if everything in the world ought to have its proper causes, there cannot be any one end which is produced from two ways of working on distinct principles . . . Therefore we protest, and do admonish the Reader, that (in our former writings) we have concealed much, by reason of the two ways we have insinuated.[2]

In his writings, yellow gold is compared to the "shut palace of the King." This refers to the fact that ordinary yellow gold is almost impossible to break down or dissolve into smaller particles. It resembles an impregnable fortress.

The only acid that can dissolve gold is produced from a combination of hydrochloric and nitric acids, which since ancient times has been called *aqua regia*—the "royal water," or "water of the king." This acid can be used to bathe gold, causing it to dissolve. As such, aqua regia is one way to open the otherwise shut palace of the king, so that the treasure of "our gold" hidden inside the palace can be discovered.

In effect, "our gold," or the seed of gold, corresponds to a very finely divided form that no longer displays the physical, chemical, or electrical properties of ordinary metallic gold. The fact is that when a metal, or any solid, becomes broken down into finer and finer parts, corresponding to micro-clusters of atoms, the properties displayed by the solid begin to disappear. This fundamental phenomenon was described in a *Scientific American* magazine article in the following manner:

> Divide and subdivide a solid and the traits of its solidity fade away one by one, like the features of the Cheshire Cat, to be replaced by characteristics that are not those of liquids or gases. They belong instead to a new phase of matter, the micro-cluster. Micro-clusters consist of tiny aggregates comprising from two to several hundred atoms. They pose questions that lie at the heart of solid-state physics and chemistry, and the related field of material science. How small must an aggregate of particles become before the character of the substance they once formed is lost? How might the atoms reconfigure if freed from the influence of the matter that surrounds them? If the substance is a metal, how small must this cluster of atoms be to avoid the characteristic sharing of free electrons that underlies conductivity?[3]

As discussed in the preface to this volume, during the 1980s David Hudson and his metallurgical chemists discovered a new and previously unknown form of gold and the platinum-group elements, which are naturally produced within the earth and spewed out in volcanic eruptions.

They discovered that this new form of gold and the platinum-group elements consists of monatomic forms of these precious metals, which consist of single atoms whose electron orbitals have been reconfigured or rearranged. This is the ultimate form of a micro-cluster—which consists of a single atom. In fact, it is not a micro-cluster at all. It is a mono-atom. The net effect is that the atoms become reconfigured; their electron orbitals become rearranged. As a result, they become chemically inert, incapable of interacting chemically with other substances, and incapable of being identified using standard assay or spectroscopic methods. In his patent filings, Hudson thus referred to these elements as ORME, an acronym for orbitally rearranged monatomic elements.

When in an ORME state, gold no longer appears as ordinary yellow gold. It appears as a white powder, as fine as hoarfrost or talcum powder, that no longer possesses the physical, chemical, or electrical properties of metallic yellow gold. The single atoms of gold that constitute this white powder were referred to by the alchemists as the "seeds of gold." When yellow gold is transformed into this powder, they called it "our gold." The only way to obtain this type of gold is to open the doors to the shut palace of the king—that is, to break down bulk yellow gold into finer and finer particles.

The Wet Way

The white powder of gold not only exists naturally in the ores of gold, especially in volcanic ores, but Hudson demonstrated that it can also be produced artificially using wet chemistry. A similar methodology was recognized by Philalethes and earlier medieval alchemists, who called it the Wet Way (Via Humidia).

Although his writings on the subject are somewhat obscure, in Philalethes's day (seventeenth century), the methods for producing both hydrochloric and nitric acids, as well as aqua regia, were well known. When chemists dissolve metals or other substances in acids to obtain solutions, this is commonly called wet chemistry. To break down gold into finer particles using wet chemistry, the alchemists employed aqua regia. That is also the methodology outlined by Hudson in his patent filings.

Normally, when gold is dissolved in aqua regia, it breaks down into smaller clusters consisting of several hundred to several thousand gold atoms, which still retain the properties of metallic gold. Once the gold has been dissolved, it can then be precipitated from the acidic solution by means of a base (such as sodium hydroxide) and reconstituted in the furnace as bulk metallic gold. This process of dissolving, precipitating, and reconstituting gold has been used for centuries as a means to purify gold from any base metals that it might be alloyed with. In this well-known process, no one has ever observed the white powder of gold.

Hudson and his chemists, however, discovered that there is a way to produce the white powder of gold using aqua regia. But the process requires salt (ordinary sodium chloride), and it also requires patience. I myself have performed this process on numerous occasions and can testify as to its validity.

The procedure is relatively simple. It is laid out in Hudson's patents, albeit in a somewhat obscure manner. All one has to do is to dissolve a specific quantity of yellow gold in a specific quantity of aqua regia and then eliminate the nitric portion of the acid to obtain a hydrochloric solution. One must then add a proper proportion of salt and allow the solution to continuously digest for at least three months over a low heat, replenishing the hydrochloric acid as needed. The sign of success is obtained when the hydrochloric solution, normally a golden yellow, turns to a beautiful emerald green—and remains that color whether the acid solution is concentrated or dilute, hot or cold. One may also observe in the green solution a white flocculent, which resembles dissolved tissue paper.

This result is not normally observed in hydrochloric gold solutions, because salt is not used, and because the solutions are not typically digested over continuous heat for three months. The green color begins to appear only after two months, and becomes stable only after three months. The process thus requires patience—a virtue all would-be alchemists must have in abundance.

Sodium hydroxide can be used to precipitate the gold from the green solution. But when sodium hydroxide is used, one will not obtain the hydroxide of ordinary gold, which is brown in color. Rather, one will obtain the hydroxide of monatomic gold, which is snow white in color.

When the precipitate is filtered, dried, and then annealed in a furnace to eliminate the hydroxide and oxide forms of the material, one obtains pure ORME gold. This pure ORME gold cannot be dissolved in any acid, including aqua regia, and cannot be reduced back to an ordinary metallic state in any fire less than 5,000 degrees Celsius in the presence of carbon.

The materials and means to perform this first part of this procedure were readily available in Philalethes' time. Among European alchemists, a great deal of emphasis was placed upon the use of salt. In fact, those who promoted the Wet Way held that the three primary alchemical ingredients were gold, mercury, and salt. Without the use of salt, the Wet Way simply won't work. Without the addition of salt, you can digest a hydrochloric solution of gold forever and it will not turn green, and the precipitate will always be brown.

Upon attaining the white powder of gold from the solution in this manner, the yellow gold is literally gone. It cannot be recovered from the solution. The only precipitate one can obtain is the white powder of gold. But when sent out for standard assay, the precipitate will show no gold at all! This happens because the properties of gold have radically changed. The atoms have been reconfigured—their electron orbitals have been rearranged. It is no longer ordinary gold; it has become philosophic gold, or the seed of gold, which the alchemists called "our gold."

There is a problem with this process, however, which would have proved a stumbling block for the alchemists. To obtain pure white gold from the white hydroxide of gold, the material must be annealed in a controlled atmosphere, first under hydrogen and then under argon. Today this can easily be done using a tube furnace and gases provided by any gas supply company. But the ancient alchemists did not have access to electric tube furnaces or pure gases. As a result, they had to work with the white hydroxide of gold obtained as a precipitate from the hydrochloric solution.

This is not nearly as effective for the alchemical work as pure white gold. Hence, the Wet Way was not deemed the best way, nor was it deemed the most ancient way. In fact, according to Philalethes, the white powder (gold hydroxide) obtained by alchemists following the Wet Way would not and cannot produce the elixir at all. It was promoted by pretenders to the work, or by those who sought to mislead the unwary. To produce the elixir one needs the pure white powder of gold—not the white hydroxide of gold.

The Dry Way

There is no mention in Hudson's patent filings of another way to produce the pure white powder from the metals, other than the way described, which requires annealing the white hydroxides in controlled atmospheres. The ancients did not have access to this technology—so how could they possibly have produced the pure white powder of gold?

It turns out that they had a completely different methodology, one that did not involve wet chemistry and did not require the use of high-temperature furnaces and controlled atmospheres. It involved the use of metals alone, under conditions of relatively low temperature. Philalethes referred to this as the Dry Way (Via Sicca), and claimed that this was the ancient way, the only way that had been used since time immemorial.

The Dry Way is called "dry" because it does not involve wet chemistry, or the use of acids. It does, however, require the use of antimony. Antimony is a dry, brittle metal that can be easily shattered by hitting it with a hammer. It has a melting temperature about the same as lead, and when melted looks just like liquid mercury. Both mercury and antimony played an important role in early gold production and refinement, because both are capable of dissolving gold.

At ordinary room temperature, mercury is already in a molten state, such that it appears as a liquid. If you were to place a gold coin in a pool of mercury, the coin would slowly dissolve over time, forming an amalgam with the mercury. But this is not a quick process. It can take days or weeks for a gold coin to fully dissolve in a jar of mercury. Nevertheless, because mercury has the potential to dissolve gold, the ancients compared it to an acid. But mercury is not really an acid; it is a pure metal. To use an analogy, it can be compared to a dry acid.

When antimony is melted, it also has the potential to dissolve gold, forming a molten alloy. But it is much more efficient at dissolving gold than mercury. One can take some crushed antimony, place it in a steel spoon, and hold it over a candle flame until the antimony melts. If one then places some yellow gold in the spoon along with the antimony, the gold will dissolve into the molten antimony right then and there, like an ice cube dissolving in warm water. I know this for a fact, because I have done this experiment myself.

For this reason, the ancients often compared antimony to a voracious wolf, which has the potential to quickly devour gold. In fact, antimony is probably the most efficient dissolver of gold known to man—more efficient than even aqua regia—and therein lies its usefulness in opening the shut palace of the king and producing our gold.

The ancients developed an ingenius method to produce both monatomic (single-atom) and diatomic (two-atom) forms of pure gold using antimony. When gold is in a monatomic form, it appears as a fine white powder, and when it is in a diatomic form, it appears as a fine red powder. The alchemists referred to these as "white sulfur" and "red sulfur," respectively. But these were no sulfurs at all; they were monatomic and diatomic forms of pure gold. They were compared to "sulfurs" because both have the potential to congeal, or fix, mercury, like ordinary sulfur.

Anyone who has seen a suspension of colloidal gold cannot help but notice its beautiful purple color. This is because the micro-clusters of gold suspended in the liquid give off purple light. As the clusters are reduced in size, such that they contain fewer and fewer atoms, the light becomes increasingly red. It becomes the purest red imaginable when the clusters consist of only two gold atoms. This was the red pigment used in the gorgeous glass murals of the medieval European cathedrals, such as the Cathedral of Notre Dame, built by the Knights Templar. It was made by fusing the red sulfur, or diatomic gold, into molten glass to give the glass a lustrous, rich red color.

The Templars, who were reputed to possess secret alchemical knowledge, were the only ones who knew how to make this unique colored glass, which had such a lustrous red color. After they were persecuted by a nefarious collusion between the French king and the pope, their knowledge was lost. Ostensibly, they made their pigment using the old dry way, which involves the use of antimony to create finely divided forms of gold.

As far as can be gleaned from the works of Nicolas Flamel, a noted fourteenth-century European alchemist, and Philalethes, the procedure is not that complicated. First, ordinary yellow gold must be dissolved in molten antimony and allowed to digest over low heat for a certain, but unspecified, period of time. Once the proper period has elapsed, the alloy is to be taken out of the vessel, allowed to cool, crushed, and then mixed with liquid mercury. Unlike gold, antimony will not form an amalgam with the mercury. It cannot be wetted by mercury.

Upon grinding the mixture using a pestle and mortar, the antimony will evolve out of the liquid mercury as a fine black powder. The alchemists referred to this as the dregs of the black dog, or the dregs of the voracious gray wolf (antimony), which can be easily washed away with pure water. Once the mercury is pure and free from any antimony powder, it will be laden with the finely divided micro-clusters of gold that were previously alloyed with the antimony.

The mercury is then to be placed in a retort and distilled. When all of the mercury has gone over into the receiving vessel, a lump of yellow gold will remain behind in the bottom of the retort. But if one's materials, procedures, and time periods are correct, the gold at the bottom of the retort should be less than the amount of gold that one started with. According to the texts, the finest parts of the gold will "fly" with the mercury into the receiving vessel, while the dross remains behind.

The liquid mercury (and finely divided gold) in the receiving vessel is then set aside and stored for future use. The dross of gold is then dissolved in a new batch of molten antimony, and the process repeated. In each repetition, the antimony-gold alloy is mixed with the stored liquid mercury-gold amalgam. The mixture is then ground, washed, and redistilled as before. The alchemists referred to each such repetition as an "eagle."

After seven to ten eagles, or repetitions, the mercury, which is now laden with very finely divided micro-clusters of gold, is placed in a sealed vessel and digested over low heat for an extended period of time. Again, patience is required. Eventually, either a white or a red powder, or a mixture of the two, will evolve and float on the surface of the liquid mercury. This powder consists of monatomic (white) or diatomic (red) forms of pure gold.

The ancients collected these powders with a feather and stored them for future use. These were known as the white and red sulfurs, both of which were viewed as philosophic forms of "our gold." This was the ancient way used to "open the shut palace of the king" and obtain the mysterious philosophic gold.

Unlike the wet way, which requires various acids and bases as well as controlled atmosphere furnaces, the dry way requires simply antimony, mercury, and gold, and some rudimentary equipment, which could even be fashioned using clay pots. As such, it could, at least in principle, have been practiced thousands of years ago, long before modern acids, bases, and tube furnaces were developed.

The information presented here is solid. It demonstrates that the alchemists were not just a bunch of quacks, with no real knowledge of the metals and their workings. But they were not just ordinary metalsmiths either. Their work required both art and patience. Neither the wet nor the dry way can be accomplished in a day's time. They both require months of patient practice.

Philosophic Mercury

Philosophic gold is one of the two main ingredients used to produce the fabled elixir. The other main ingredient was called philosophic mercury. Alchemy was commonly called the Royal Art. In this context, philosophic gold was compared to a king, whereas philosophic mercury was compared to a queen. To begin the great work (magnum opus), the king and the queen had to be united in an alchemical marriage. The alchemical child born from this union, over the course of nine to ten months, was none other than the miraculous elixir.

Ordinary metallic mercury and ordinary metallic gold are not sufficient to produce the result. Both have to be properly prepared for their alchemical marriage; they have to be rendered "philosophic." In both cases, the alchemists tell us that antimony is required.

The process used to prepare the philosophic mercury is substantially different from that required to prepare the philosophic gold. As in the case of philosophic gold, ordinary liquid mercury must be mixed with antimony, and the mixture heated until a molten suspension is obtained. As in the case of philosophic gold, over a period of time a dry powder is supposed to evolve from the molten metals, which then floats on the surface. But unlike the gold preparation, this powder is not red or white. It is supposed to be a forest green. Moreover, it has no use; it can be discarded.

The greenness that blossoms on the surface of the liquid metal closely resembles a plant, like an alga. Using plant symbolism, this was called the royal herb, which was likened to a moss that grows on a bog. Using animal symbolism, it was called the green lion. In both cases, it was not the royal herb or green lion itself that was of use—rather, it was the sap of the herb, or the blood of the lion, that was of supreme importance. In the Vedic tradition, that sap or blood was called *rasa,* a Sanskrit word that simultaneously means sap, juice, blood, and mercury. It corresponds to the liquid metal that lies below the green powder. This is the philosophic mercury.

Mercury was called quicksilver, or living silver, because it has the potential to blossom into greenness—the color of vegetable life—when made philosophic. To accomplish this miracle, the ancients held that ordinary mercury must become infused with the Holy Spirit—namely, the spirit (kohl) of antimony. The quickening, or greening, of mercury is the sign that it has become philosophic.

In actuality, this greenness consists of a fine green powder that evolves out of the mercury and floats on its surface. But the powder is forest green only when the mercury is hot. If the material is allowed to cool, it turns gray.

The dry powder itself is of no use. It is merely a sign that the mercury has been properly prepared. It is not the green lion that is important, it is the blood of the green lion. It is not the royal herb that is important, it is the sap of the herb.

Once this sign has been observed, then the entire material is to be taken out of the vessel, allowed to cool, and crushed using a mortar and pestle. When crushed, the sap (philosophic mercury) will ooze out of the herb. The resultant liquid is to be filtered through a wool cloth until the juices come out bright and shining, like pure quicksilver. To remove any hidden particles of the powder, the liquid can be distilled.

In the Vedic tradition, this fully purified form of philosophic mercury was called rasa. It represents the queen that is to be married with the king in the sealed alchemical vessel. The elixir born in the vessel from the nine- or ten-month rite was then called amrita rasa—the nectar of immortality, which both immortals and mortals seek to obtain.

The preparation of philosophic mercury was considered an even more profound secret than the preparation of philosophic gold. Although the process described above sounds simple, there are hidden secrets involved. You can go out and purchase pure antimony and pure mercury from a chemical supply house and attempt to replicate this process—but you will never see the sign. You will never see the greening or quickening of the mercury no matter how long the mixture is digested. I know, because I have tried it. There is something else involved, which by the grace of God, I discovered after months of ardent practice and study. This is a secret that has never before been revealed in any written text. I will reveal it to you toward the end of this book, but you have to be patient.

To put this discovery in context, I refer to the words of Eirenaeus

Philalethes, who was viewed as the last great master of the art and whose writings Newton studied assiduously. Like other alchemists of his time, Philalethes expressed his teachings using an alchemical code language. In his writings, the liquid mercury hidden under the green powder was compared to the doves of Diana (the Greek moon goddess). In alchemical traditions around the world, metallic mercury was traditionally symbolized by the moon (*luna,* or soma). Because it occurs as a liquid that can be distilled, or made to "fly," Philalethes referred to the philosophic mercury using the code words "Diana's Doves." The green powder that floats on top of the philosophic mercury, and which embraces the philosophic mercury in its arms, was symbolized by Venus, who was the Greek goddess of spring—and hence the goddess of greenness.

In his typical benevolent manner, Philalethes wished the secret of philosophic mercury upon those worthy of receiving it and sought to disclose the secret, albeit in the following veiled terms:

> We have made and do possess the Stone, the great Elixir, nor verily will we envy thee the knowledge thereof, but we wish that thou mayest learn them from these writings. We have likewise declared, that the preparation of the true Philosophical Mercury is difficult, the main knot lying in finding Diana's Doves [the philosophic mercury], which are folded in the everlasting arms of Venus [the green powder], which no eyes but a true philosopher ever saw. This one skill performs the mastery of theory, ennobles a philosopher, and unfolds to the knower of it our secrets. This is the Gordian Knot, which will be a knot forever to a Tyro in the Art, except the Finger of God direct, yea so difficult that there needs to be a particular grace of God, if anyone would obtain the exact knowledge thereof.[4]

Through the grace of God, I have discovered this secret and have witnessed the greening of mercury. Let me state clearly that the process needed to obtain the philosophic mercury in no way conflicts with that described previously. But you cannot use pure antimony obtained from a chemical supply house to achieve the result. You must obtain the antimony by performing the Star Regulus, as has been done for thousands of years. Therein lies the secret, which I have yet to fully reveal.

Like Philalethes, I too wish to bestow this secret upon the reader and will do so toward the end of this book—in simple, unveiled, scientific terms. But I will not do so to a "Tyro in the Art." To obtain the secret, you will have to wade through this book and learn the true importance of the ancient art and science, such that hopefully you will become a master of theory. Then I will tell you the secret, such that those of you who wish to pursue the art can also become masters of practice.

A Word to the Wise

Let me give a word to the wise. Do not even think about performing the processes described in this book if you are not a competent metallurgist with an approved laboratory and appropriate safety equipment, such as a ventilation hood and air-filtration system. Mercury and antimony fumes are highly toxic—they will kill you (or turn your brain into swiss cheese) if you inhale them.

Newton's strange psychotic behavior late in his life has been attributed by some to antimony and mercury poisoning. Back then the toxicity was not clearly understood, and he subjected himself to the fumes over the course of years. History tells us that many would-be alchemists have died from pursuing the art. You have been forewarned. Neither I nor the publishers of this book take any responsibility if you attempt to perform the processes described herein without proper knowledge, supervision, and equipment. The ancients compared mercury to a serpent. The serpent may guard a vast golden treasure, but its breath and venom can be deadly. Don't let it bite you.

The Alchemical Marriage

The procedures and methodologies outlined above do not constitute the magnum opus, or great work, of the alchemists. They are merely the preliminary steps that must be taken to properly prepare the king (gold) and queen (mercury) for their alchemical marriage.

Once the philosophic gold and mercury have been obtained, then the king and queen must be properly married within the alchemical vessel. Unlike ordinary metallic gold, the seeds of gold cannot be wetted by mercury. Monatomic gold will not form an amalgam with mercury. The same thing holds true for diatomic gold. That is why the white and red powders of gold evolve out of the mercury and float on the surface during the preparation.

According to Philalethes, either the white or red powder can be used to perform the marriage, with similar results. Once again, the procedure is relatively simple. The philosophic gold is to be mixed with the philosophic mercury to form a "Rebis"—a mixture of two different things, with opposite properties. In this case, the opposite properties are dry and wet. The proportions should be such that the mixture has the consistency of bread dough.

Getting the philosophic gold to mix with the philosophic mercury in this manner requires some work. The Rebis can be achieved either by grinding the two materials together in a mortar and pestle or by placing the mixture in a jar and shaking it vigorously. Both processes require a long time and a substantial amount of labor. In the end, a dry-wet suspension is achieved, such that the mixture of the two materials obtains a more or less homogeneous nature. This is the Rebis. But if the Rebis is allowed to sit for too long, the two materials will separate. Thus, it must be prepared immediately before the marriage takes place.

Once the Rebis has been prepared, the mixture is to be quickly placed in a hermetically sealed vessel and subjected to moderate heat. That is all. This effects the alchemical marriage. There is nothing else to be done by the hand of man. Then the magnum opus, or great work, begins—and it is conducted by the hand of God alone.

The Magnum Opus

The great work serves to give birth to the alchemical child—the elixir—which is born from the union of the king and queen. This does not happen immediately. It is a long, slow process that takes nine to ten months of continuous digestion. This is the same time frame required to give birth to a human child, from the union of its father and its mother.

As in the human case, once the union takes place, the whole process of gestation and development within the womb (or vessel) is carried out by the hand of God, without any intervention from man.

In the human case, all that is required is to maintain the female vessel by feeding her food and drink. In the alchemical case, all that is required is to maintain the fire that heats the vessel by feeding it fuel.

During the gestation period, the two materials go through a series of transformations, noticeable by changes in consistency and color, until they are no longer two materials but a single uniform and homogenous elixir, the color of congealed blood, which is unlike anything on earth.

> At the last by the will of God, a light shall be sent upon thy Matter, which thou canst not imagine; then expect a sudden end, within three days thou shalt see, for thy Matter shall convert itself to grains, as fine as the atoms of the sun, and the color will be the highest Red imaginable, which for its transcendent redness will shew blackish, like unto the soundest blood when it is congealed, although thou mayest not believe that any such thing can be an exact parallel of our Elixir, for it is a marvelous Creature, not having its compare in the whole Universe, nor any thing exactly like it.[5]

Although the resultant elixir was called a stone, it was not a stone at all. Rather, it was a fixed and incombustible powder:

> Know, then, that it is called a stone, not because it is like a stone, but only because, by virtue of its fixed nature, it resists the action of fire as successfully as any stone. . . . Its appearance is that of very fine powder, impalpable to the touch, sweet to the taste, fragrant to the smell, in potency a most penetrative spirit, apparently dry and yet unctuous, and easily capable of tinging a plate of metal. It is justly called the Father of all miracles, containing as it does all the elements in such a way that none predominates, but all form a certain fifth essence; it is thus well called our gentle metallic fire . . . If we say that its nature is spiritual, it would be no more than the truth; if we described it is as corporeal, the expression would be equally correct; for it is subtle, penetrative, glorified, spiritual gold. It is the noblest of all created things after the rational soul, and has virtue to repair all defects both in animal and metallic bodies, by restoring them to the most exact and perfect temper; wherefore is it a spirit or quintessence.[6]

To obtain this miraculous spiritualized form of matter, the material must course through various stages, where it assumes a black, white, green, citrine, and finally a dark red color. The final stage, when the material assumes a dark red color, was variously called the philosopher's stone, or elixir, which both gods and immortals seek to obtain, calling it amrita rasa—the immortal blood. This is the true holy blood (sang réal) contained in the Holy Grail (san gréal), and we are on a modern-day quest to obtain it.

Plant Symbolism

Although the practice of alchemy was rooted in solid metallurgical principles, the application of those principles to achieve the desired result required some degree of art, skill, and patience. Alchemy was not just a secret science; it was also a secret art. As Philalethes put it:

> But these things are so set down by obscure philosophers to deceive the unwary, as we have before spoken; for is not this an *ars cabalistica* or a secret and a hidden art? Is it not an art full of secrets? And believest thou O fool that we plainly teach this secret of secrets, taking our words according to their literal signification?[7]

The alchemical code language employed alchemical symbols. There were two basic types of alchemical symbolism, which can be called plant symbolism and animal symbolism. First, let's examine the roots of the plant symbolism.

European alchemists often referred to the development of the elixir as the growth of the Hermes Tree, which vegetates or grows from the seeds of gold planted in philosophic mercury, often compared to waters. A literal interpretation leads to the speculation that the elixir was produced from plants. But Philalethes denied this notion and insisted that the true elixir was derived from the metals, not from plants.

> Our Tree is Metalline, and yet through the power of God it seems to Vegetate.[8]

The elixir was compared to the Hermes Tree, because the Greek god Hermes was viewed as the father of Western alchemy. Hence, alchemy was commonly understood as the Hermetic art, and the airtight vessels used to perform the work were described as hermetically sealed.

The Greek wisdom god Hermes corresponds to the Semite wisdom god Sin, the Egyptian wisdom god Thoth, and the Vedic wisdom god Soma. All of these were viewed as lunar deities. In this regard, the philosophical mercury, which served as the principal ingredient of the elixir, was commonly referred to as *luna*—the moon. The Hermes Tree may thus be understood as the "moon plant"—the plant that grows from luna, or philosophical mercury.

This is not to be confused with the "royal herb" or "green lion" discussed earlier, whose sap or blood gives rise to the philosophical mercury. The Hermes Tree represents the elixir itself, which grows from the seeds of gold placed in the philosophical mercury over the course of nine or ten months.

One of the first-known Western alchemists, who was revered during the Hellenistic era as a great master on the subject, was Maria the Jewess. It is from her that we have the *bain-marie*—a French term that refers to a double boiler, used to heat one pot by placing it in another pot that is filled with water and heated.

According to ancient accounts, Maria's work pertained to a "white, clear, and precious herb, which grows on the small mountains."[9] Some have speculated that this "white herb" was *Botrychium lunaria,* otherwise known as moonwort—or the moon plant.[10] But this involves a literal interpretation, which is contrary to the alchemical symbolism involved.

As noted previously, the seven ancient metals were commonly symbolized by seven planets and seven mountains. The "small mountains" described by Maria the Jewess thus correspond to small mounds of the metals, such as gold and mercury, from which the elixir—the metallic herb, plant, or tree—grows. It was described as "white" because according to all the alchemical traditions, the white form of the elixir, also known as the Medicine of the First Order, represents the first "resurrected" form of the metals to appear during the magnum opus. That "whiteness," which resembles the color of the moon, lay at the basis of the lunar symbology.

The mysterious moon plant associated with Maria the Jewess is synonymous with the Vedic soma plant, where the word *soma* simultaneously means the elixir and the moon. Hence, moon plant = soma plant. A Sanskrit synonym for the word *soma* is *rasa,* which among other things means metallic "mercury" and "blood."

The use of plant symbolism to describe metallurgical materials and processes follows a general homology between the practice of alchemy and the practice of agriculture. According to the ancient theory, the metal ores grow in the earth like plants. Thus, the veins of metallic ore found embedded in the mountains were often compared to stalks, veins, and branches of a metallic plant or herb growing on or in the mountains.

The practice of agriculture involves collecting the seeds obtained from the natural plants and then planting them in a properly prepared ground, allowing them to be warmed by the heat of the sun, and watering them. The actual growth of the plants then occurs miraculously, without any laying on of hands. The final result is ordinary food, which can be ingested to nourish the body.

Similarly, the practice of alchemy was said to involve collecting the "seeds of metals" from the natural ores, which grow in the earth like plants. The metallic seeds were then planted in a vessel filled with the mercurial water and warmed by the heat of the fire. If the materials and regimen of the fire were correct, then the elixir was supposed to grow in the vessel miraculously, without any laying on of hands. The final result was the food of the gods, which can be ingested to nourish the mind and soul.

This homology lies at the basis of the ancient and ubiquitous use of plant symbolism to encode secret alchemical processes all around the world. There is no doubt, of course, that the ancients also used plants and herbs to produce various medicinal elixirs. But the practice of plant alchemy was deemed a lower form of the art, often referred to as "the lesser work." The practice of metallic alchemy, which involved the use of metals alone, was deemed the great work (magnum opus) from which the true elixir of immortality was obtained.

This symbolism is the key to uncovering the hidden meanings in the ancient myths. For example, in the *Rig Veda,* the soma was said to be obtained from the soma plant, which grows on the rocks of the mountains. But this was no ordinary plant at all. It was a metallic plant, consisting of veins of metal ore embedded in the mountains.

The idea that the Vedic description of soma is actually an alchemical allegory has already been suggested by various Vedic scholars. Dr. S. Kalyanaraman, a Vedic scholar and author of an authoritative dictionary on ancient languages, recently published a book titled *Indian Alchemy: Soma in the Veda,* in which he presents a detailed analysis of the Vedic mantras, demonstrating their hidden metallurgical meanings.

For example, Kalyanaraman cites ancient references that suggest the soma was obtained from two rocks, which had a golden (*harita*) and red or purplish (*aruna*) color. These correspond to quartzite gold, which is golden in color, and cinnabar (mercury sulfide), which is red or purplish in color—two of the raw materials required for the work.

The Vedic texts state that the *kavis,* the alchemical priests who actually made the soma, purchased the raw materials for their work from the Mujavats. According to Kalyanaraman, the Mujavats were ancient tribes that lived in the mountainous regions of Afghanistan. This is the closest region to the Indian subcontinent where there are naturally occurring sources of cinnabar.* It is also known that that same region was once part of the ancient Indus-Sarasvati civilization, which some believe to have been the early Vedic civilization.

But this type of plant symbolism was not unique to the Vedic tradition. In the Sumerian myths, the elixir of immortality was described in terms of a mysterious "plant of life," and in the book of Genesis it was described in terms of a mysterious "Tree of Life."

Animal Symbolism

In addition to plant symbolism, the ancients also used animal symbolism. This was because the final elixir was viewed as a conscious form of matter, resembling a living being. A living being is conceived by planting male seed in a female womb, which is then nourished by the feminine fluids and energy and the warmth of the female body. Over the course of several months, the seed develops into an embryo and then a

---

*Although cinnabar is mixed with other ores throughout the trans-Himalayan region, the nearest source of concentrated naturally occurring ore cinnabar to the Indian subcontinent is Garmshir (Pir Kisri) in Afghanistan.[11]

living being, which is finally delivered from the womb. Once again, this occurs miraculously without any laying on of hands.

The unique feature of a living being is that it is conscious. It represents a form of matter that has been infused with consciousness, or spirit, such that it becomes a living form of matter—a living being.

By analogy, the alchemical vessel was compared to the female womb in which the masculine seeds of gold were to be sown. The liquid mercury within the vessel was then compared to the feminine fluids, and the heat of the fire was compared to the warmth of the female body—both of which serve to nourish the seeds and engender their growth into the divine embryo, the sacred elixir, which was deemed a conscious form of matter—that is, a "Creature," or a living being.

This symbolism is also related to the notion that the development of the elixir within the vessel was said to take nine or ten months, just like the development of a babe in the womb. This time frame is very ancient. It was the time frame specified not only by the Western European alchemists, such as Philalethes, but also by the Vedic seers.

The kavis, who were assigned the duty of producing the soma, and the great sage Angiras, in particular, who was credited as being the first to teach his followers how to produce the soma, were thus described in the *Rig Veda* as the practitioners of the nine- or ten-month rite.[12]

Although the myth of Angiras is little known in the West, his name has been preserved in Indo-European languages around the world. Etymologists have determined that the original Sanskrit word *angiras* became *angiros* in Old Persian, *angelos* in Greek, *angelus* in Latin, and *angel* in English. Thus, Angiras may be viewed as the prototype for what we now call an angel. This goes back to the Hellenistic myth that the science of alchemy was originally revealed by the fallen angels—that is, the angels, gods, or godlike sages who descended to Earth in the predawn history of the human race.

Although the elixir was viewed as a synthetic substance, produced by man, the alchemists viewed themselves as little more than the nursemaids of nature. They argued that they employed in their alchemical procedures the same basic process used by nature to develop the metals within the body of the earth, plants from the body of the earth, and living beings from female wombs.

By the application of their art and science, the natural processes were accelerated, so that the metals were able to rapidly obtain their apotheosis as the most fully evolved form of matter possible—a form of matter that is infused with consciousness, and which, when ingested, is capable of nourishing the spirit or consciousness of man and rendering the soul immortal.

According to the ancients, these natural processes are ultimately governed by spiritual processes involving the self-interacting fields of consciousness that transcend all means of direct empirical observation. As such, their "science" extended beyond the scope of ordinary physical science. It was literally a science of consciousness and its relationship with matter.

Conclusion

In this chapter, I have attempted to present an overview of the ancient art and science of alchemy as I understand it, based upon my own practical experience and intuitive reading of the ancient texts. In the chapters that follow, I will examine how this ancient art and science was viewed at various times in history and in different cultures. In the process, I will demonstrate that the sacred art lay at the very heart of some of the most ancient and enduring cultures the Earth has ever known.

I start with the medieval European tradition, because the European alchemists' viewpoints were more closely related to our modern scientific perspective than were the more ancient viewpoints. The European alchemists thus provide a convenient transition between very ancient and modern times.

TWO
European Alchemy

The Influx of Alchemy into Western Europe

The practice of alchemy in Europe, especially in Spain, in the Pyrenees mountains between Spain and France, and in southern France, may have been a continuous tradition since Hellenistic times. But if so, it was largely an underground tradition.

Gold can be found throughout the world. But mercury (or cinnabar) deposits are more restricted. It thus seems reasonable to presume that ancient alchemical cults formed around sources of cinnabar.

The cinnabar mines at Almaden, Spain, located about 200 kilometers south of Madrid in the Brown Mountain Range, have been in continuous operation since Roman times and are the most prolific sources of liquid mercury in the world, even today. An estimated 250,000 metric tons of liquid mercury have been obtained from these mines over the past two thousand years, about one-third of the world's entire historical production. Even as early as AD 1200, the mines were at a depth of 450 feet and employed more than a thousand workers.

The Romans used the mercury coming from Spain in their gold-mining operations around the empire. They perfected the art of leaching gold from crushed ore by soaking the ore in large vats of liquid mercury over a period of time, and then draining off the mercury and distilling it to obtain the gold dross left behind.

When the Moors invaded and occupied Spain, between the eighth and thirteenth centuries, the cinnabar mines came under Arabic control and the mercury was used for medicinal, alchemical, and continued metallurgical purposes. After the fall of the Roman Empire, most of western Europe was controlled by the Roman Catholic Church, which tended to ban any books or treatises from pre-Christian times. The Arabic nations, however, were not controlled by the church, and ancient traditions of alchemy, dating back to at least the Hellenistic era, persisted in those regions and were carried with the Moors to Spain.

During that time, there were also several Jewish communities in northern Spain and southern France, which had been there for several hundred years. Like the Brown Mountains farther south, the Pyrenees had also been a source of cinnabar since ancient times, with another large mine located at Tarna, in northern Spain. The Jewish people had been linked with alchemical practices since at least the Hellenistic era. In fact, the first notable Western alchemist in the historical record is Maria the Jewess. Zosimos of Panopolis, one of the earliest Greek writers on the subject, in the fourth century AD makes it clear that he considered the Jewish people repositories of alchemical wisdom.

> In a remarkable passage he says that the sacred art of the Egyptians (that is alchemy) and the power of gold that resulted from it were revealed only to the Jews . . . and they made it known to the rest of the world. In general Zosimos held that the Jews' knowledge of alchemy was greater and more reliable that that of any other people, including even the Egyptians [of the time].[1]

The Jewish communities in southern France, such as in Toledo, were renown for their mystical teachings of the Kabbalah and were suspected by the Roman Catholic Church and others of alchemical practices. This was the same region that the Cathars or Albigensian sect of Christian heretics, also suspected of secret alchemical practices and often linked with the Holy Grail legend, surfaced in the eleventh century. They reportedly possessed a treasure worth more than all the gold in the world, which they kept hidden in their mountain strongholds, where a number of Knights Templar fortresses were also built around the same time.

The Cathars appear to have had Gnostic roots. They believed that the human spirit has the potential to communicate with God directly, without the need for any human intervention, such as that provided by the pope, and were a peace-loving people who practiced both meditation and vegetarianism. In addition, they allowed their "pure ones," or teachers, to be either male or female, unlike the church, with its male-dominated attitude, which was rooted in Roman culture.

For a time persons involved in alchemy were in danger of being burned at the stake. In the twelfth century, Pope Innocent III initiated a crusade against the Cathars by inviting armies from all over northern Europe to invade southern France and wipe out the sect with his blessings. He promised the armies all the land that they conquered and all the wealth they could take by force from these helpless people, who were considered heretics in the eyes of the pope.

At one point, when a crusading general had surrounded a large city and asked for guidance, the pope told him to kill them all, no matter what they professed, because God would know his own.[2] So several hundred thousand people were killed, sometimes by being burned at the stake, for their beliefs contrary to church doctrine. This marked the early beginnings of the Inquisition, which terrorized Europe for several hundred years and resulted in an estimated two hundred thousand women, suspected of witchcraft, herbalism, or alchemy, to be burned at the stake.

Early alchemical influences came not only from Spain and southern France but also from the Middle East through eastern Europe. For more than a thousand years, a secretive Hermetic cult known as the Sabeans thrived in Harran, an ancient city often mentioned in the Bible, which still exists in Turkey today. Turkey, or ancient Anatolia, had also been a source of cinnabar since ancient times. The Hermetic sect there appears to have been linked with the practice of Hermetic alchemy, presumably dating back to the Hellenistic era, when the Hermetic texts, the sacred texts of the Sabeans, were composed.

Around the time of the first Crusade, the Sabeans were kicked out of Harran by Islamic fundamentalists and migrated farther west into eastern Europe, where their texts and alchemical ideas began to circulate. This eventually gave rise to the Hermetic tradition of European alchemy, which was similar in theory and practice to the Jewish and Moorish traditions arising in Spain and southern France.

Another early group suspected of alchemy were the Knights Templar, an order of Christian monks founded during the first Crusade, which delivered Jerusalem back to Christian Roman control for the first time in almost a thousand years. Upon their return from the Middle East, the Templars quickly rose to become the wealthiest and most powerful Christian order of the time. Among other things, they developed the first international banking system, involving the issuance of chits, or pieces of paper, which could be carried anywhere and cashed in for gold deposited at the Templar strongholds around Europe. There are those who believe that the Templars' sudden rise to power and wealth were due partially to secrets that they uncovered while in Jerusalem, secrets that are sometimes considered to be of an alchemical nature.

In 1307, about a century after the Albigensian crusade in southern France, the Templars themselves came under persecution by the Church, which accused them of heresy, homosexuality, and secret practices forbidden by the Church. On the morning of Friday, the thirteenth of October 1307, the French king, who was essentially a vassal of the pope, moved against the Templars at their strongholds all across France, snuffing out the entire order in a single day. Ever since that time, Friday the thirteenth has been considered an unlucky day.

In 1314, after seven years of horrendous torture at the hands of the Inquisitors, the grand master Jacques de Molay and six other remaining leaders of the Templars were burned at the stake for the public's amusement, at the behest of both the pope and the French king. While being burned, de Molay reportedly cursed the pope, who then mysteriously died a year later.

Three years after de Molay's death, in 1317, the new pope John XXII issued a papal bull against the production of alchemical gold, and as a result the Cistercians banned alchemy. In 1323, the Dominicans in France followed with a general ban and ordered the burning of all known alchemical documents.

In spite of this general ban, it appears that a number of clerics secretly pursued alchemy within the confines of their monasteries. Even though Pope Benedict XII ordered an investigation into the alchemical activities of some clerics and monks in 1339, the practice appears to have continued within certain monastic orders, without any serious prosecutions. In 1376, however, the Dominican textbook for Inquisitors placed alchemists among magicians and wizards—which meant they were doomed for destruction. As a result, the practice of alchemy went completely underground; practitioners became highly isolated or maintained their links with one another through secret societies.

Even at the time of Philalethes (seventeenth century), the life of an alchemist was not an easy one. Although the actual identity of Philalethes is unknown, according to his own testimony he came from a well-to-do family, was introduced to the art by a master of the work, and succeeded in making the great elixir for the first time himself at the age of twenty-four. From that time forward he was a marked man; he had to divorce himself from his family and friends and pursue a fugitive lifestyle. In this regard, he compared his plight and that of his fellow alchemists to the plight of Cain.

> We judge ourselves to have received (as it were) the curse of Cain . . . We are driven, as "twere from the Face of the Lord," and from the pleasant society which we heretofore had with our friends . . . nor can we suppose our selves safe, in any one place long. We often-

> times take up . . . the Lamentations of Cain unto the Lord, "Behold whosoever shall find me, shall kill me." We travel through many Nations, like Vagabonds, and dare not take upon us the care of a family, neither do we possess any certain habitation.[3]

From time to time, various European rulers also banned the practice of alchemy, fearing that the alchemical production of silver and gold would threaten their economic power. Decrees banning the practice of alchemy were thus issued in 1380 by King Charles V, and later by King Henry IV in England. Although the royals were opposed to the public having this knowledge, they were also keenly interested in exploring this possibility for themselves. A number of European monarchs thus commissioned or licensed certain individuals to pursue alchemical research under their oversight, sometimes torturing or executing those who failed in their quest.

The European alchemists thus viewed themselves as under siege by both secular and religious authorities. Nevertheless, they persevered, with the belief that they possessed a supreme secret, hidden from the eyes of the world since the beginning of time, which had the potential to confer enormous riches and power upon those who learned it. But they believed that only those who were pure of heart and who had renounced the riches and power of this world deserved to possess their secret.

The symbolic and often confusing nature of the alchemical texts has proved a serious stumbling block for those seeking to replicate the work. According to Philalethes, many of the alchemical texts were written by charlatans, who had no real knowledge of the work and only sought to impress their investors.

As a result, the practice of alchemy in western Europe has a checkered history. It was generally the work of isolated individuals, working in secret, who often published their writings anonymously or under pseudonyms out of fear for their lives. Although many European alchemists came from well-established and wealthy families, they pursued their art in secret and lived beyond the pale of accepted society. They treaded the dangerous waters of new ideas, which often involved a revival of ancient knowledge other than that espoused by the church. Their secrecy and isolation from one another, as well as the lack of any organized historical tradition, bred a hodgepodge of terminology and practice that ultimately led to widespread confusion and a loss of the knowledge.

The Alchemists and Their Texts

Robert of Chester, an English scholar, appears to have been the first to translate an Arabic work of alchemy into Latin (*De composition alchemiae*), sometime around AD 1140–50. He was followed by Gerard of Cremona (AD 1114–1187), an Italian scholar living in Toledo, Spain, who is credited with translating ninety-two Arabic works of alchemy into Latin. Early European alchemists included Artephius, Albertus Magnus, Roger Bacon, Arnold of Villanova, Raymond Lully, Nicolas Flamel, Bernard of Treviso, and Sir George Ripley, all of whom composed their own texts, often in Latin.

In the mid- to late-1400s the Italian Renaissance began to flourish under the patronage of Cosimo de' Medici, who commissioned the translation of the *Corpus Hermeticum* and the works of Plato and Plotinus from Greek into Latin. The Hermetic teachings, which claimed Egyptian heritage, were rapidly absorbed into the Kabbalistic and Christian schools of alchemy, giving rise to many different branches of alchemical thought, which thrived during the sixteenth and seventeenth centuries throughout Europe—in Germany, France, England, Austria, and Italy. During this period, numerous charlatans, pretenders, and would-be alchemists wrote treatises and sought funding for their unsuccessful alchemical experiments, giving the art a bad name.

Isaac Newton was the last notable scholar to devote himself to the serious pursuit of alchemy. He made a careful study of the works of Eirenaeus Philalethes, who is believed to be the last great master. But Newton was ultimately unsuccessful in obtaining the goal. After that, alchemy became increasingly unpopular in scholarly circles, having been replaced by modern chemistry.

Whether or not the European alchemists ever actually achieved their goal is unknown. What is known is that from around the fourteenth century, the pursuit of alchemy became a suitable cloak for fraud. A number of impostors who claimed to have achieved the great work began to appear on the scene, and using various tricks such as hollow stirring rods loaded with gold, they proceeded to soak their investors for all they were worth. Others wrote spurious documents, on a purely theoretical basis with no real knowledge of the process, even though they claimed to be adepts. Consequently, by the end of the seventeenth century, the whole art and science of alchemy had fallen into disrepute and began to be eschewed by a growing consensus of scientists.

The distinction between ancient alchemy and modern chemistry became firmly established by Robert Boyle (1627–1691), who first postulated and then demonstrated the existence of indivisible chemical elements, such as oxygen, carbon, and so forth, through the formulation of the stoichiometric laws of chemical combination. This culminated in the death of alchemy, which held that all forms of matter were of a common fluid essence and could be transmuted into one another under certain conditions. It wasn't until the twentieth century that the common units (subatomic particles) of all of the chemical elements were finally understood.

Modern scholars now recognize that the practice of alchemy was literally the precursor to modern *chemistry,* a word that is derived from the same origins. In their pursuit of the philosopher's stone, the European alchemists developed a number of procedures, methodologies, and formulae that continue to be used today in both metallurgy and chemistry. But the idea that a secret elixir can be produced from the metals, capable of expanding consciousness, extending longevity, and enhancing health, as well as transmuting base metals into gold, is not part of modern chemistry or metallurgy.

Transmuting Base Metals into Gold

The myths and legends that surround the original form of alchemy, practiced by the earliest cultures on earth, suggest that its primary purpose was to obtain the elixir of immortality to be used for spiritual purposes. When the practice resurfaced in medieval Europe, a different emphasis was placed upon it. The pursuit of alchemy became synonymous with the pursuit of the philosopher's stone, which could be used to transmute base metals into gold.

Such transmutations were not unknown to the ancients. In the alchemical tradition in India known as *rasavidya* (science of *rasa*), there was an ancient aphorism:

> *Yatha lohe, tatha dehe*
> [As in the metals, so in the body.]

The Indian alchemists first tested the elixir on the metals to determine whether it was both safe enough to be ingested and potent enough to render the soul immortal. If the elixir (or rasa) was capable of transmuting the base metals into gold, then it was deemed safe to ingest and capable of rendering the body free from disease and the soul immortal.

But there is no indication in the rasavidya texts that alchemy was pursued for the sake of obtaining a vast wealth of gold. The focus was entirely spiritual. The transmutation was simply viewed as a test to determine the validity of the elixir, which was to be used for spiritual purposes and not wasted in the production of gold.

The Europeans turned this ancient perspective on its head. The vast majority of European practitioners pursued alchemy to obtain a wealth of gold, not to obtain spiritual immortality. European monarchs banned the practice of alchemy in order to prevent their currency, based upon a gold and silver standard, from becoming debased, and any form of gold that was deemed alchemically produced was banned as currency.

With the advent of Robert Boyle's theory of indivisible chemical elements and the stoichiometric laws of chemistry, the idea that the base metals, such as lead and mercury, could be transmuted into gold became viewed as farcical and ridiculous, and the pursuit of alchemy rapidly died away. It was not until the twentieth century and the development of nuclear physics that the possibility of nuclear transmutation became a recognized fact.

Low-Energy Nuclear Transmutation

The lead and mercury atoms must emit alpha particles from the nucleus, such that their atomic number becomes reduced, in order for nuclear transmutation to occur. As far as is known, the only way for this to happen is via thermonuclear fission, a process that requires extremely high energies or temperatures, such as those found at the heart of the sun. The idea that such transmutations can take place at temperatures ordinarily produced by fires and furnaces is not accepted.

In 1995, however, I was personally invited to the first conference on Low-Energy Nuclear Transmutation, hosted by Dr. John Bokris, a distinguished professor of chemistry at Texas A&M University in Austin. In attendance were reputable scientists from countries around the world, such as Japan, Russia, Europe, and the United States, including the Los Alamos (New Mexico) National Laboratory, where the first atomic bomb was developed. A representative from the U.S. Department of Energy was also in attendance, in the hopes that attendees might have discovered some new method to produce tritium, a necessary ingredient in atomic bombs. In one presentation after another, the scientists shared their evidence of low-energy nuclear transmutation.

The typical experiment presented at the conference involved starting with a given set of materials whose elements were carefully assayed, putting them through a low-energy chemical or electrical process, and then assaying the results. The scientists found that during the process some of the elements disappeared and new ones appeared in their place, or that the ratio of elements changed.

These results imply that the elements underwent a process of nuclear transmutation—at low energies. The results, however, are totally anomalous. They cannot be explained on the basis of standard nuclear physics, which requires thermonuclear temperatures for such transmutations to occur.

Although an appropriate theory has yet to be developed that could account for such low-energy transmutations, the evidence that such transmutations can occur is already established. This is consistent with the ancient myths and legends surrounding the elixir, or philosopher's stone, which was deemed capable of effecting such transmutations in a low-energy process.

The Fluid Theory of the Nucleus

In the ancient alchemical theories, the possibility of nuclear transmutation was attributed to the fluidlike nature of the metals—the belief that all of the metals have their basis in a mysterious fluidlike substance that percolates from the center of the earth and from the center of every metal atom. By operating on the level of this fluidlike substance, it was held that one metal could be transmuted into another metal even at low temperatures.

The ancients did not mean the molten forms of the metals, which can indeed assume a fluidlike character. Rather, they were talking about something deeper, a hidden fluid essence of the metals that could congeal into the form of different metals under different conditions. This implies that they were talking about the atomic nucleus, which determines the identity of a metal, or any atomic element in general.

Over the course of the last decade or so, a new theory of the atomic nucleus has begun to emerge based upon a superfluid model. The idea is that the protons and neutrons in the nucleus constitute a coherent, condensed state of matter whose behavior resembles that of a quantum fluid, or a superfluid, which can deform elastically, like a fluid drop having a certain surface tension. This nuclear drop model is now on the forefront of nuclear physics, and provides a completely new way to look at the structure of the nucleus and nuclear reactions. Although the theory is still in its infancy, it may very well hold the key to understanding the process of low-energy nuclear transmutation.

In this case, ancient alchemical theory and modern nuclear physics may ultimately come to agree on the notion that one metal can be transmuted into another by operating on the hidden fluid essence of the metal, that is, the nuclear drop, at relatively low temperatures.

Eyewitness Accounts of Transmutation

Although eyewitness accounts of alchemical transmutation are few and far between, two accounts were provided: one by John Frederick Helvetius, an eminent doctor of medicine and physician to the prince of Orange during the seventeenth century, the other by John Baptist von Helmont, a physician in Brussels during the sixteenth century. In what follows we present a synopsis of the account provided by Helvetius, which is on record in The Hague.[4]

According to his testimony, on the afternoon of December 27, 1666, Helvetius was visited at his home by an unannounced stranger with an air of authority dressed in the garb of a Mennonite. Apparently Helvetius had previously published works against the possibility of alchemy, and the stranger had come to set him straight.

The stranger took out a carved ivory box that contained three large pieces of what appeared to be amber-colored glass or resin, and informed Helvetius that this was enough of the Tincture (the form of the stone prepared for transmutation) to produce twenty tons of gold. At the conclusion of his narrative, Helvetius asked him to prove his assertion, but the stranger demurred and told him that he would return in three weeks time, and if he were at liberty to do so, he would then demonstrate the power of the Tincture.

When the stranger returned three weeks later, he informed Helvetius that he was not able to fulfill his request because it had been conditional upon his receiving permission (ostensibly from his own master) to perform the transmutation. Helvetius implored him to at least give him a small piece of the Tincture so that he could investigate it for himself. The stranger then gave to him—as though it were the most "princely donation in the world"—a piece of the matter no bigger than a grape seed.

When Helvetius argued that this tiny amount could not possibly tinge or transmute more than four grains of lead at the most, the stranger demanded that he give back the material. Helvetius complied, thinking that he would exchange it for a larger piece, but instead the stranger divided it in two with his thumbnail and gave him half as much as before, telling him, "Even now it is sufficient for you." Helvetius was disappointed, for he could not imagine that this tiny amount of material would be able to do anything.

The stranger then instructed him to take half an ounce of lead and melt it in a crucible, for that was the proper quantity for that amount of the stone. Helvetius subsequently confessed to the stranger that he had managed to steal a few crumbs from his ivory box on his last visit and had experimented with them, but they had done nothing but change his lead into a glassy substance.

The stranger laughed, and told Helvetius that he was more adept as a thief than as an alchemist. He explained that he should wrap the Tincture in a ball of wax before casting it on the molten lead, so that it might penetrate the lead more thoroughly. After promising to return the next morning, the stranger departed. The next day he did not show up, and Helvetius's wife implored him to try the transmutation himself. He decided to proceed.

> I then cast the Tincture, enveloped as it was in wax, on the lead; as soon as it was melted, there was a hissing sound and a slight effervescence, and after a quarter of an hour I found that the whole mass of lead had been turned into the finest gold. Before this transmutation took place, the compound became intensely green, but as soon as I had poured it into the melting pot it assumed a hue like blood. When it cooled it glittered and shone like gold. We immediately took it to the goldsmith, who at once declared it to be the finest gold he had ever seen, and offered to pay fifty florins an ounce for it.[5]

The rumor of Helvetius's success spread like wildfire through the city. That afternoon he had visits from many illustrious students of alchemy, and also received a call from the Master of the Mint and some other gentlemen, who requested that he give them a small piece of the gold so that they might subject it to a standard assay.

Helvetius consented and they went to the house of a silversmith named Brechtil, who submitted a small piece of the gold to a standard fire assay, in which the gold is mixed with silver and beaten into thin plates, which are then dissolved in nitric acid. This dissolves the silver and any other base metals, leaving the gold in the form of a black powder at the bottom of the dish. This black powder is then put into a cuppel and heated in a furnace, at which point the gold is reconstituted.

When they performed the assay, they discovered that not only had they recovered the full weight of the gold, but two scruples of the silver had also undergone a change into gold. In other words, they obtained more gold than they started with! Apparently some of the Tincture was still active in the gold and had acted upon the silver as well. They repeated this test three more times, and each time the gold was increased by a scruple. Although everyone was amazed at these results, the stranger never came to visit Helvetius again, and as a result the transmutation could not be repeated.

The Effervescence

The important thing to note about the testimony of Helvetius is the hissing and effervescence reported at the time of transmutation. In the other eyewitness account, reported by John Baptist von Helmont, it was said that when the transmutation took place there was a "certain amount of noise."

From modern nuclear physics we know that it is indeed possible to transmute lead into gold—by releasing alpha particles (helium nuclei) from the lead nucleus through a process of nuclear fission.

If the transmutation of lead into gold reported by Helvetius and von Helmont involved a low-energy form of nuclear fission, then the alpha particles would have boiled off as a gas, which (if it happened suddenly) would undoubtedly have created a "hissing" sound as the vapors escaped, along with an "effervescence" of the molten metal.

But they could not possibly have known this fact because nuclear physics did not exist at the time. Did Helvetius actually witness a low-energy process of nuclear transmutation, involving the sudden release of alpha particles? Once again, this suggests that the myths and legends surrounding the practice of alchemy may actually have a scientific basis.

The Phases of the Great Work

Once the materials of gold and mercury have been properly prepared, and thus made "philosophic," they are then mixed together and placed inside a sealed vessel for a continuous process of digestion extending over many months. The progress that occurs inside the sealed vessel is marked by various color changes, which are supposed to take place within certain time frames. The following description of the various phases of the great work and their corresponding periods was provided by Philalethes.[6]

For the first forty days or so, the material endures what may be called the "flood," as the mercury vapors rise, condense, and then fall like rain onto the waters below. This was called the phase of Mercury.

After the first forty days the "rains" begin to abate as the material enters into the dissolution phase. During this phase the liquid matter begins to decompose and dry up into a fine bluish black powder, emitting dark vapors that fill the vessel. The vapors that ascend above were called the "breath of the dragon," and the black powder that remains below was called the "head of the crow." This was called the phase of Saturn.*

The peak of blackness is reached around the ninetieth day, after which the darkness begins to abate. But it is not banished until 150 days have passed, at which point the water is supposed to completely dry up and the dark clouds cleared. Around that time, the matter is supposed to turn into a fine snow-white powder—the color of the purest milk. This was called the phase of the Moon. At that stage, the material was variously called the White Stone, the Milk of Life, the Virgin's Milk, or the Medicine of the First Order. According to Philalethes, this white form of the elixir is not only safe to ingest but also capable of curing all ills.

But the white phase does not represent the end of the process. During the white phase the material first appears as a fine white powder, which afterward begins to fuse and liquefy. It will purportedly sublime or volatilize if the fire is too great. During this phase, the material appears as white cream, which gradually begins to sprout into a translucent greenness, which is referred to as the phase of Venus.

After about seven and a half months of continuous digestion, the matter is said to turn a beautiful citrine, or amber color, which was called the phase of Mars. Finally, the amber color becomes penetrated by a violet or purple color, and then within a period of about three days

*At this stage the matter is deadly poisonous. Indeed, mercury vapor at any stage in the process is highly toxic—and nothing described herein should even be attempted by one who is not a knowledgeable metallurgist.

it turns into a dark vermilion color, resembling congealed blood. This final phase, which occurs during the ninth or tenth month, was called the phase of the Sun. It marks the completion of the process. But the alchemist is not yet finished.

Multiplication

Upon first attaining the red elixir it should resemble a fine powder, the color of congealed blood. But the powder obtained at the end of nine months does not represent the fully perfected form of the elixir.

In order to achieve final perfection, it must undergo another process, called multiplication. This involves putting the red elixir back into a new batch of philosophic mercury for another round of black, white, green, yellow, and red transformations, which takes about twenty-eight days (a philosophical month) rather than nine months. Through this process both the quantity and potency of the elixir was said to be increased.

Apparently, this process can be reiterated as many times as one likes. But each time the process of multiplication is repeated, it comes to completion in a shorter and shorter period, and there is a logarithmic increase in the potency of the elixir. In this manner, a small initial quantity of the elixir may be quickly transformed into a large quantity and its potency enhanced.

The Perfected Elixir

The perfected form of the elixir, or stone, is described below:

> Having thus completed the operation, let the vessel cool, and on opening it you will perceive your matter to be fixed into a ponderous mass, thoroughly of a scarlet color, which is easily reducible to powder by scraping, or otherwise, and in being heated in the fire flows like wax, without smoking, flaming, or loss of substance, returning when cold

> to its former fixity, heavier than gold, bulk for bulk, yet easy to be dissolved in any liquid, in which a few grains being taken its operation most wonderfully pervades the human body, to the extirpation of all disorders, prolonging life by its use to its utmost period; and hence it has obtained the appellation of "Panacea," or a Universal Remedy.[7]

This description makes it clear that the final elixir could assume many forms. When cold it can assume a fixed form resembling hardened resin. In this light, it was compared to a stone—namely, the philosopher's stone. But because the stone can easily be converted into a powder by scraping or grinding, it was also described as an elixir (powder). Over and above these two solid forms of the material, it could also assume a liquid form, by either subjecting it to heat or dissolving it or, more accurately, suspending it in any liquid. In some ancient traditions the sacred elixir was thus compared to a drink, while in others it was compared to a solid food. Without the insight provided by the later European texts, it would be natural to view these different forms of the elixir as completely different substances.

The Healing Power of the Elixir

With respect to ingesting the elixir, the European alchemists were very wary. They report that many practitioners died in the process of trying to ingest the elixir—either because their elixir was false and thus poisonous or because they took too much and died because of its enormous, and thus overwhelming, transformational power.

The prescribed dose was to take a tiny grain of the stone and dissolve it in alcohol or water until the liquid attained a red color, resembling red wine. Then one should take a drop of this liquor and place it in another jug of water or alcohol, which would be less red. This process should be continued until the liquid obtains a golden color. This was called "potable gold." In one passage it is said that one should take a few drops of this golden liquor every few months to maintain perfect health and freedom from disease. Philalethes describes the powerful effect of the elixir as though it were a veritable fountain of youth:

> A man or woman who is born to hereditary weakness, may be changed into a more than ordinary strength by the use of our Medicine; or a man who by labour, sickness, and years, is come to Grave's mouth, even to drop in it, may by use hereof be restored his hair, his teeth, and his strength, so that he shall be of greater agility than in his youth, and of greater strength, and may live many years, provided the period of the Almighty's decree be not come.[8]

The Projection Powder

In addition to consuming the elixir, the European alchemists claimed that it could also be used to transmute base metals into gold. To accomplish this, one first had to prepare a red-gold glass by fusing the red elixir with pure gold in a furnace. Below are Flamel's instructions for this process, recorded in his *Breviary.*

> Here is this procedure. Melt in a crucible 10 ounces of fine gold and throw in it, on the melted gold, one ounce of the red powder. Leave it in a very strong fire for two hours, remove the crucible, let it cool, break it, and you will see in the bottom a red glass, that is the exalted gold, true and royal powder capable of transmuting all metals into pure gold, better than the one found in the mines.

The instructions then direct the practitioner to grind the red-gold glass into a powder, called the projection powder, and store it in a sealed vessel. When one desires to make gold from lead or mercury, one should then heat the lead until it becomes molten, or in the case of mercury until it begins to fume, and then throw in the projection powder of red-gold glass wrapped up in a ball of wax. Flamel claimed that five or six grains of the projection powder will transmute thirty or forty pounds of lead or mercury into the finest gold.

Flamel also claimed that, depending upon how many cycles of multiplication the elixir has been put through, its ability to transmute the metals may increase dramatically. In one passage, he claims that thrice-multiplied elixir has the potential to transmute approximately one hundred thousand times its weight of base metals into pure gold. As an interesting side note, he stated that the gold obtained through this method will actually weigh slightly less than the mercury or lead that one started with.

As discussed previously, it is a scientific fact that both mercury and lead can be transmuted into pure gold. But according to modern science, this can be accomplished only through a high-energy process of nuclear fission, involving the release of alpha particles (nucleons). Because both mercury and lead have a higher atomic number than gold, if one were to start with a certain quantity of lead or mercury and transmute the entire mass into gold (through a process of nuclear fission), then the gold obtained would necessarily weigh slightly less than the original mercury or lead due to the emission of alpha particles—exactly as claimed by Flamel.

The problem is that Flamel lived in the fourteenth century, when nuclear physics was completely unknown. Is it possible that the projection powder somehow catalyzed a low-energy process of nuclear fission in the mercury or lead, thus transmuting the base metal into pure gold?

As in the Beginning, So in the End

With respect to the actual production of the elixir or stone, there is a great deal of confusion, which revolves around similarities between the starting materials and the final products of the process. Virtually all of the European alchemists agreed that one of the starting materials is a specially prepared form of metallic mercury called philosophic mercury. The other starting material was a specially prepared form of gold called "our gold," or philosophic gold.

As discussed earlier, the philosophic gold consists of finely divided forms of gold (monatomic and diatomic) that no longer display the physical, chemical, or electrical properties of bulk yellow gold. Rather, these two forms of gold appear as a white and red powder, called the white sulfur and red sulfur. They were compared to "sulfurs" because they have the potential to congeal the liquid mercury, like ordinary sulfur. But they were not the chemical element that we know as sulfur. They were specially prepared forms of pure gold, different from ordinary metallic yellow gold.

The problem is that the white and red sulfurs, which serve as starting materials for the work, are similar in color to the white and red forms of the elixir, which are the usable end products of the work. The ancients explained this similarity by the aphorism "As in the beginning, so in the end."

The white and red sulfurs constitute the seeds of gold from which the elixir grows in the vessel, like a plant, with no intervention from humans. The entire material first turns black, then white, then greenish, then yellowish, and finally red. These are precisely the colors associated with the production of the *soma* in the *Rig Veda.*

In the rasavidya traditions of medieval India, these colored elixirs were denoted by the term *abhraka,* which generally means "stone," although it is commonly translated as "mica," a type of silicate stone. Four types of abhraka are mentioned, colored white, green, yellow, and red. The Arabic myth that the door to a vast treasure of gold could be opened by speaking the words "*abhraka dabhra*" may be directly linked to the rasavidya tradition, in which the Sanskrit words literally mean "a little bit (dabhra = dab) of the stone (abhraka)." As discussed above, the alchemists believed that only a tiny dab of the stone is enough to produce a large quantity of gold.

Any of the colored elixirs were deemed suitable for human consumption, because the "metallic" nature of the gold and mercury was viewed as having died during the phase of blackness (dissolution), such that the metals no longer displayed their former chemical or metallic properties, and thus were no longer toxic.

Particular importance was placed upon the white and red elixirs, which were deemed food for the body and spirit, respectively. The white elixir, which comes before the red, was thus called the Medicine of the First Order. But to obscure their teachings, the alchemists purposefully wrote in a confusing manner, such that in a given discussion one is not always sure whether they are talking about the white and red sulfurs that serve as the starting materials or the white and red elixirs that serve as the end products. This confusion between the beginning and the end has served as a stumbling block for many who have tried to replicate the work.

Superheavy Elements

According to Philalethes and others, the final product of the alchemical process, that is, the final red elixir, is homogeneous in nature, such that it no longer consists of gold and mercury but of a single homogeneous element, which was believed to be unlike any element found on Earth. The European alchemists claimed that this unique and mysterious element was much heavier, bulk for bulk, than ordinary yellow gold.

This presents a serious problem, because there is no element known to man that is much heavier than gold, bulk for bulk. Osmium and some of the radioactive elements are slightly heavier than gold by bulk density, but not by much. If we take the word of the alchemists at face value, this leaves only one possibility. The red elixir must be composed of *superheavy elements,* unlike anything that naturally exists on Earth.

The existence of superheavy elements, whose atomic numbers exceed the known atomic elements, is recognized in nuclear physics. In fact a great deal of current nuclear research is focused on synthesizing such elements in high-energy nuclear reactors.

According to nuclear physics, the nucleons within the nucleus are organized into nuclear shells resembling, at least in certain respects, the electron shells that constitute the outer portions of the atom. The theory predicts that at around atomic numbers 114–115 there should be a nuclear shell closing, which will render the superheavy atom nonradioactive and as stable as any of the known stable atoms, with an expected half-life of more than half a billion years.

Although attempts are under way, especially in Russia, to synthesize such elements using high-energy bombardment techniques, the scientists have had little success to date. Any superheavy elements created in the reactors tend to rapidly decay, by means of nuclear fission, to more-stable forms of atomic matter.

Is it possible that the ancients possessed a low-energy, low-tech method of synthesizing stable superheavy elements by means of their alchemical process? That is the only possible answer to the question: What form of matter might be much heavier than gold, bulk for bulk?

Clearly, the ancients did not have sophisticated nuclear reactors, nor did they have a sophisticated mathematical theory of the atomic nucleus. But the ancient sages and seers did have extraordinary powers of intuition and claimed the ability to intuitively cognize whatever exists, on any scale of time and space.

If the transmutation of lead or mercury into pure gold requires a low-energy process of nuclear *fission,* then the production of the elixir itself will require a lower-energy process of nuclear *fusion,* in which the gold and mercury atoms are broken down and reconstituted as superheavy atoms, with a much higher atomic number.

Is there any empirical evidence of this type of fusion, which operates at low energies? The answer is: maybe. In the late 1980s two electrochemists at the University of Utah made headlines around the world with their claim to have discovered a low-energy process of nuclear fusion known as "cold fusion."

Because subsequent experiments demonstrated that their process was unreliable and difficult to replicate, the majority of scientists concluded that it was not a real phenomenon. Nevertheless, research continues to be performed by a small but very vocal minority of scientists, who claim that the phenomenon of cold fusion is real and should be investigated further. Is it possible that the mechanism that underlies the process of cold fusion is related to the mechanisms of alchemy?

The Elixir Is Not a Drug

Some may attempt to draw parallels between the elixir and various psychotropic drugs. But if the elixir is anything like ORME, then it cannot be viewed as a drug, because ORME, once annealed, is chemically inert. Unlike yellow gold, the pure-white powder of gold cannot be dissolved in aqua regia, or in any of the other known acids or bases. It simply doesn't react chemically—not at all. Unlike a drug, or a chemically active substance, ORME gold cannot react chemically in the body. It can be *suspended* in a liquid, like a colloidal suspension, but it cannot actually be *dissolved* in a liquid.

Therefore, the mechanism by which the ORME-type elements produce an effect on the body and mind must be nonchemical. The effect must be a matter of physics, or, more appropriately, metaphysics, rather than a matter of chemistry. According to the ancients, the effects of the elixir are due to the nonlocal influence of consciousness, which is the ultimate source of all bodily and mental intelligence.

Even if the U.S. Food and Drug Administration were to rule that ORME gold is a drug, due to its bodily and mental effects, the FDA would find it impossible to regulate, due to the fact that ORME is impossible to identify using ordinary laboratory procedures or assay techniques. As a result, the white powder of gold could be mixed with any ordinary substance, and only the ordinary substance alone would show up in a lab analysis. The white powder of gold itself would escape detection.

If the elixir is anything like the ORME gold, in accordance with the principle "As in the beginning, so in the end," then it is highly likely that it too will be chemically inert, and thus not a drug. Wouldn't it be ironic if the ultimate cure-all for bodily, mental, and spiritual disease turned out to be a drug-free material consisting of chemically inert superheavy elements—unlike any element found on earth? That is precisely the promise offered by the ancient theory and practice of alchemy.

THREE
Jewish Alchemy

Biblical Code Language

In his scholarly work *The Jewish Alchemists: A History and Source Book,* which cites hundreds of historical documents, Raphael Patai notes that in the Western traditions there is "scarcely a single important work on the [alchemical] science, which is not directly related to the Jews, with their tradition and their science."[1] Therefore, let's examine the Jewish tradition of alchemy.

One of the earliest Hellenistic writers on the subject, known to scholars as Pseudo-Democritus (ca. 100 BC), suggested that the Jews described and exposed the practice using a "secret language.

> The Jews alone have attained a knowledge of its practice, and also have described and exposed these things in a secret language.[2]

The notion that the Jews described their knowledge of alchemy using a secret language resurfaced in medieval Europe when "it became fashionable to write alchemical commentaries to the first verses of Genesis, and to derive alchemy from them."[3] The first few chapters of Genesis, in particular, were looked upon by many as alchemical allegories, in which the creation of the universe pertains to the creation of the elixir, the Tree of Life symbolizes the elixir, the time periods associated with the Great Flood pertain to the phases of the work, and so on. Consider the following long title of one European alchemical treatise: *The Glory Of The World: Table Of Paradise; A True Account Of The Ancient Science Which Adam Learned From God Himself; Which Noah, Abraham, And Solomon Held As One Of The Greatest Gifts Of God; Which Also All Sages, At All Times, Preferred To The Wealth Of The Whole World, Regarded As The Chief Treasure Of The Whole World, And Bequeathed Only To Good Men; Namely: The Science Of The Philosopher's Stone.*

This illustrates the notion, common among European alchemists, that the biblical patriarchs and their direct descendants formed a line of alchemical sages. In the book of Genesis, we note that the first son of Adam and Eve was called Cain (Hebrew: Kayin). The original Hebrew word literally means "metalsmith." In this regard, the Freemasons held that the biblical story of Cain is much more than what it seems on the surface, and viewed the descendants of Cain as a line of master craftsmen. It should be recalled that the European alchemists often viewed themselves as having the curse of Cain.

One of the descendants of Cain was Tubal-Cain, who was described in the Bible as a master of all blacksmiths and those who work in copper. Tubal-Cain is also invoked in the rituals associated with the rank of master freemason. There are some who have argued that the Romans later deified Tubal-Cain as the god Vulcan (Vul-Cain), who was the patron deity of vulcanism, or of all those who work with metals in the fire. It is from the Latin word *vulcan* that we have the English word *volcano.* As discussed earlier, we know that the monatomic seeds of the metals can be produced artificially, by means of both wet and dry chemistry, but they are also produced naturally in the body of the earth and spewed out in volcanic eruptions. In this sense vulcanism is also linked with the practice of alchemy.

In ancient times it was unthinkable that a son should adopt a different profession from his father. Hence, if Cain was a metalsmith, then so were his descendants, such as Tubal-Cain. But this also works in reverse. If Cain was a metalsmith, then so was his father, Adam.

The book of Genesis tells us that Adam was fashioned by the Jehovah Elohim from the "dust of the earth." In turns out that the Hebrew word *adam* literally means "red earth." Interestingly enough, the word *adam* is phonetically similar to our modern English word *atom.* If you were to have asked the medieval alchemists "What are the atoms of red earth?" they would have replied that they are the atoms of the red elixir, the stone of the philosophers. In this allegorical sense, Adam can be viewed as the very embodiment of the elixir itself, which flowed in his blood and in the blood of his descendants.

This is also the meaning of the Sanskrit name Angiras, who is credited as the first to teach the art and science of producing the amrita rasa, the elixir of immortality, to his descendants. The word *angiras* can be derived from *angir* (limb) + *rasa* (blood or elixir). The descendants of Angiras were called the *angirasas.* They were deemed a line of great sages who had the immortal blood, or sacred elixir, flowing through their limbs.

The Bible also tells us that Eve was fashioned from the "rib" of Adam. The rib cage can be viewed as the "vessel" made of bone that contains and protects the blood of the heart. In this symbolic sense, Eve may be understood as the holy vessel, or Holy Grail (san gréal), that contained the holy blood (sang réal). She was the vessel by means of which the holy blood, filled with atoms of red earth, was passed down from Adam to his descendants.

The "secret language" ascribed to the Jews can thus be understood as an alchemical code language in which the words of the Bible are not meant to be taken for their literal significations but as symbols that encode a hidden knowledge pertaining to the art and science of alchemy. If you take the Jewish calendar at face value, it puts Adam and Eve in the Garden of Eden around 4000 BCE. Apparently, this is where the Jewish tradition of alchemy began.

The Trees of the Garden

The story of the Garden of Eden revolves around the mysterious Tree of Life, which is placed front and center in the garden. The text tells us that those who taste of the Tree of Life obtain eternal life and thus become immortal. It also tells us that Adam and Eve were instructed by the Elohim (lords or gods) to till the garden and care for it. This is typical alchemical code language, which employs plant symbolism to encode alchemical or metallurgical secrets. Let's try to make sense of the story in an alchemical context.

The "Tree of Life" is symbolic of the sacred elixir, which serves as the food of the gods—that is, the food of the Elohim. Adam and Eve were forbidden to taste it lest they become like the gods and obtain eternal life.

They were also forbidden to taste of the Tree of Knowledge. The "Tree of Knowledge" is symbolic of the theoretical and practical knowledge required to actually produce the elixir. In other words, it represents the knowledge of alchemy—which the gods forbade Adam and Eve to possess.

Who were these mysterious "lords" or "gods" of the garden, and why did they deny Adam and Eve access to both the knowledge of alchemy and the elixir produced by it? It lies beyond the scope of this volume to even attempt to answer these questions in detail. Suffice it to say that Adam and Eve were not alone in the garden. They were the vassals, and possibly part-blood descendants, of the lords of the garden—the mysterious Elohim.

In this context, Adam and Eve played the role of common laborers, employed by an elite ruling class (the Elohim), who were viewed as the very embodiments of the gods on earth. As laborers, they were not actually involved in making the elixir or consuming it. Their job was to mine (till) the earth to obtain the metallic ores required for the practice. They were not allowed access to the secret knowledge of the practice or the elixir produced from it.

According to the story told in Genesis, Adam and Eve were nevertheless tempted by a wise serpent to taste of the Tree of Knowledge. The serpent was then cursed, and Adam and Eve were banned from the garden lest they "take from the Tree of Life also and obtain eternal life." What is going on here? What is the meaning hidden behind the scene?

First, let's be clear about the alchemical symbolism involved. The serpent, and especially the winged serpent, has been a potent alchemical symbol since the very beginning. The winged serpent characterizes the caduceus of Mercury, the messenger of the gods in the Roman tradition, whose counterpart was Hermes in the Greek tradition—the father of Western alchemy.

In the Sumerian tradition, which also began to take shape around 4000 BCE and in the same geographical area, winged serpents were used to symbolize the mysterious gods called the Annunaki—the sons of Anu, or the sons of heaven. In the same way that the Genesis myth tells us that the Elohim possessed the "Tree of Life," so too the Sumerian myths tell us that the Annunaki possess the "plant of life"—the mere taste of which bestowed immortality.

The myths also tell us that the early Sumerian kings, who claimed to be part-blood descendants of the Annunaki, were nevertheless denied access to the plant of life by the Annunaki, just as Adam and Eve were denied access to the Tree of Life by the Elohim. This leads to the hypothesis that the Elohim and Annunaki were the same mysterious group of godlike sages who dominated the area as the spiritual lords of the region.

Whoever these mysterious people were, they were not secular rulers hell-bent on conquest. They were spiritual rulers—or alchemical sages—who might be more appropriately compared to Merlins of the forest. They conquered not by force of arms but by their spiritual wisdom and authority, and also by arranged intermarriage, a practice quite common in ancient times. To the native inhabitants of the region, they would have been viewed as the messengers of the gods—the people of the winged serpent.

This leads to the hypothesis that the wise serpent who tempted Adam and Eve was none other than one of the wise alchemical priests, commissioned by the lords of the garden to actually make the elixir. This scenario makes sense. If Adam and Eve, and ostensibly their followers, were gathering the ores for the alchemical priests, it seems reasonable to suppose that the priests may have allowed them to hang around after delivering the ores, at which time they may have been tempted to observe the priest's alchemical practices—either intentionally or unintentionally. By doing so, they tasted the forbidden Tree of Knowledge. The priest was punished, and Adam and Eve were banished from the garden and from the presence of the lords, lest they take from the Tree of Life also and obtain eternal life.

But there was no erasing what they had seen and learned. As a result, the tradition of Jewish alchemy began. From that time forward, Adam and his descendants assumed the role of alchemical priests themselves. This is consistent with early Hellenistic commentators on the tradition of Jewish alchemy. They claimed that the Jews had obtained their knowledge of alchemy by subterfuge and then revealed it to the world using a secret language.

The Location of the Garden

There is no doubt that the myth presented in the book of Genesis is a spiritual allegory that has a deep, universal interpretation. But we would argue that it also has a historical and alchemical interpretation related to a specific location, described as the headwaters of four rivers. The pertinent passage describing the location of the Garden of Eden is given below.

> Now there was a river issuing out of Eden to water the garden, and from there it began to be parted and it became, as it were, four heads. The first one's name is Pishon; it is the one encircling the entire land Havilah, where the gold is. And the *gold* of the land is good. There

> also are the bdellium [Hebrew: *bdolach*] and the cornelian [Hebrew: *shoham eben*]. And the name of the second river is Gihon; it is the one encircling the entire land of Cush. And the name of the third river is Hiddekel; it is the one going to the east of Asshur. And the fourth river is the Euphrates.[4]

For thousands of years, speculations concerning the original location of the Garden of Eden have been put forward, but over the past thirty years or so the pieces have finally begun to fall into place. From the description given in Genesis, it should be apparent that even if the Garden of Eden has a deeper metaphysical interpretation, it also appears to represent a real place that served as the headwaters of four rivers. Two of the rivers are known. The Hiddekel is none other than the "Deglat" in Sumerian or "Tigris" in Greek. As described in the text, it runs to the east of Asshur—a city that exists even today. The Euphrates is also known and exists today.

The text implies that the Garden of Eden lay somewhere near the headwaters of the Tigris and Euphrates Rivers. These two rivers have their geographical source in the mountainous regions of Kurdistan, corresponding to northeastern Iraq, Armenia, and northwestern Iran. But what about the other two rivers, called the Pishon and the Gihon?

David Rohl, a well-known British author, historian, and Egyptologist, has suggested that these two rivers correspond to the modern-day Uizon and Aras, which originate in the same region but flow east into the Caspian Sea.[5] It turns out that Uizon = Pishon, and the old Islamic name for the Aras River is Gaihun = Gihon.

The book of Genesis suggests that the Garden of Eden was located somewhere near the headwaters of these four rivers. The actual Hebrew term for the Garden of Eden is *gan eden,* which literally means a "walled garden." This suggests that it refers to a lush hidden valley (the garden), with a river flowing through it, which is surrounded by mountains, which serve as the walls of the garden.

After studying the topography of the region and examining the ancient place-names in the area, Rohl developed a convincing theory that the Garden of Eden corresponds to what is now known as the Tabriz Valley, a lush, gardenlike valley with a river flowing through it, surrounded by snowcapped mountains, located in northwestern Iran. The river that flows east through this valley was referred to by the ancient Persians as the Medan, or Medan-el-sha, which literally means the "royal garden of the king." Even today, orchards laden with fruit trees line the river.

In the book of Genesis it is also made clear that the entrance to the garden lay to the east. It turns out that the only convenient entrance into the Tabriz Valley lies through a high mountain pass in the east. Ancient place-names in the area such as Kheru (cherubim) and Nodi (the land of nod) lend support to Rohl's theory. Moreover, the area has a rich archaeological history. It is located in a region where there are early signs of grain cultivation and animal domestication during the Neolithic period.

Genesis also tells us that the Garden of Eden was located close to certain mineral deposits. The text mentions three things: gold, bdellium, and carnelian:

> And the gold of the land is good. There also are the bdellium and the carnelian.[6]

Although many scholars have argued that the Garden of Eden was located in the marshy delta region of southern Iraq (ancient Mesopotamia), the fact is that there are no gold deposits found in that area. The mountainous regions of Kurdistan, Armenia, and northwestern Iran, on the other hand, do have such deposits, as indicated by ancient gold-panning sites along the rivers there.

This raises an important question. Why were these three minerals (gold, bdellium, and carnelian) mentioned in connection with the Garden of Eden, and what do they actually represent? Are we to imagine that these things were just mentioned in passing and have no real significance? This is highly unlikely. According to rabbinical scholars, every letter, word, and phrase of the book of Genesis was carefully crafted by Moses and his inner circle to encode secret meanings.

We note that the description of the location of the Garden of Eden, which refers to these three ores, immediately follows the first mention of the Tree of Life. Is it possible that these three minerals are related to the production of the elixir?

Gold, Bdellium, and Carnelian

As discussed earlier, alchemical traditions around the world required three starting ingredients, or mineral ores, for their secret process, namely gold, antimony, and mercury. Let's assume for a moment that Rohl's identification of the Garden of Eden with the Tabriz Valley is correct. Is there any evidence that the three alchemical ores could have been obtained from the surrounding area in ancient times? Let's examine each of the three minerals individually.

Gold. There is no hidden meaning when it comes to the gold. Genesis states that the gold was obtained from the region called Havilah, encircled by the river Pishon, and that the gold there was good. The Pishon (Uizon) runs along the base of the northern end of the Zagros mountain range. It is well known that there are gold deposits in the Zagros Mountains, and it is also known that the Uizon was an ancient source of gold.

Today the river flows past a village called Zarshuyan, which means "gold washing," indicating panning for gold in the river there. In addition, it is known that there was a gold mine at that site around fifteen hundred years ago. So the context appears consistent with the biblical description.

Bdellium (gum resin). The word *bdellium* (Hebrew: *bdolach*) literally means "gum resin." The Egyptian word for gum resin is *qmy.t,* while the name for the land of Egypt is Km.t, both of which are candidates for the origin of the word *alchemy.* The word *km.t* literally means "black earth"—and antimony ore (stibnite) is black. Is it possible that the mysterious gum resin (bdellium) is a code word for black antimony ore?

Many of the European alchemical texts also refer to a mysterious "gum." To cite just one example, consider the following passage taken from the text called *The Glory of the World,* whose long title was cited earlier.

> xvii. MUNDINUS: Learn, O imitators of this Art, that the philosophers have written variously of many gums in their books, but the substance they refer to is nothing but fixed and living water, out of which alone our noble Stone can be prepared. Many seek what they call the essential "gum" and cannot find it. I reveal unto you the knowledge of this gum and the mystery, which abides therein. Know that our gum is better than Sun (gold) and Moon (mercury). Therefore it is highly esteemed by the Sages, though it is very cheap; and they say: Take care that you do not waste any of our "gum." But in their books they do not call it by its common name, and that is the reason why it is hidden from the many, according to the command, which God gave to Adam.[7]

The "Sun" and "Moon" are alchemical symbols for gold and mercury, respectively. The text states that "our gum" is better than Sun and Moon, yet it is also said to be an essential ingredient for the production of the stone. It is a "fixed water." This leaves only one possibility, namely antimony or antimony ore, which was the third secret ingredient.

Antimony was viewed as superior to gold and mercury because without antimony, the gold and mercury, or Sun and Moon, cannot become properly prepared for their alchemical marriage and the subsequent birth of the divine child—the sacred elixir. It was viewed as containing the spirit of life, or Holy Spirit, which renders the gold and mercury "philosophic."

Some of the earliest man-made artifacts involving antimony alloys have been found in northwestern Iran. It is also known that antimony ore, or stibnite, was commonly used as a collyrium or black eye shadow among the Persians. This clearly indicates that in ancient times the area provided a source of stibnite, or antimony ore.

Carnelian. The third mineral described is commonly translated as either carnelian or onyx, both of which are semiprecious stones that can assume a dark red color. The original Hebrew word is *shoham eben,* whose meaning is uncertain. All that is known is that it signifies a "red stone." I suggest that this is a code word for *cinnabar* (mercury sulfide), which naturally occurs as a dark red stone.

The ancient Persians, who inhabited this same region, were well aware of this red stone. In fact, the word *cinnabar* originated from the Persian word *zinjifrah,* which means "dragon's blood," believed to be a corruption of the Sanskrit word *sindura.*

The oldest-known use of cinnabar in the Western world has been found not far away, at the ancient site of Catal Huyuk, which has been dated to around 6500 BC. The ancients in the region obtained their cinnabar from open deposits located in central and eastern Turkey, not far from the proposed location of the Garden of Eden. As such, the red stone now known as cinnabar would also have been available to those living in the garden.

The idea that these three substances, mentioned in connection with the location of Eden, are actually code words for the three principle ores out of which the elixir was produced is thus consistent with the naturally occurring ore deposits in the region. Did Moses purposefully mention these three things to encode a secret knowledge that links the origins of the Hebrew tradition and the location of the Garden of Eden with the practice of alchemy?

The Biblical Flood

Our next topic of interest concerns the account of the Great Flood—the story of Noah and the Ark. This tale may very well be tied to historical events that were exceedingly ancient by the time of Moses, who recalled the story. There are some who have suggested that the biblical Flood is related to a massive flooding of the Black Sea and its environs due to a rupture in the Bosporus Strait, dated to around 5000 BCE.

Such an event would have made a strong impact on the native population living in the region, and may very well have served as the historical basis for the biblical account. If so, then the timeline presented in the Bible may be off by at least a thousand years. But there is another interpretation of the Flood chronicle, which is profoundly alchemical in nature.

The first thing we note is that Moses and his inner circle, who actually wrote the narrative, were very specific in terms of the time frames involved. They didn't date the Flood to a particular year, but they were meticulous about describing the periods of days that marked the various Flood events. These time frames directly correspond to those described by the European alchemists as characterizing the phases of the work, discussed earlier.

This secret knowledge appears to be encoded in the biblical story of the Flood. The text states that "the Flood continued on the Earth for forty days."[8] This corresponds to the first phase of the alchemal process, in which the mercury vapors ascend and descend like "rain" upon the material below. The text then goes on to state that "the water gradually receded from the earth," and at the end of one hundred fifty days (five months) the water disappeared. This corresponds to the phase of blackness, when the material dries up into a black powder associated with a dark vapor above, resembling dark thunderclouds. These dark clouds ultimately disappear at the end of one hundred fifty days, when the material turns into a dry snow-white powder.

The text then goes on to say that on the seventeenth day of the seventh month the ark grounded on a mountain in Ararat. This corresponds to the appearance of the golden, or citrine, form of the elixir, known as the phase of Mars. The text states that "the water continued to recede until the tenth month, and on the first day of the tenth month the tops of the mountains could be seen."[8] This is the time frame for the production of the final red elixir, the culmination of the process, compared to the emergence of the Sun.

In this manner, the authors of Genesis appear to have indicated the period of wetness (forty days), the drying up of the waters and the appearance of the white stone (one hundred fifty days), the appearance of the amber or golden form of the stone (seven months, seventeen days), and, finally, the appearance of the true stone, or red elixir, which marks the pinnacle of the work (first day of the tenth month). Although one might argue that this is just coincidence, the text then goes on to describe the twenty-eight-day period required to multiply the quantity of the stone and increase its potency.

In the book of Genesis the process of multiplication is signified by the release of four birds to fly over the waters and determine the extent of dry land. The release of each bird is associated with a period of seven days. The first bird released was the raven, indicating the seven-day period of blackness. The second bird released was the dove, indicating the seven-day period of whiteness. The third bird released was another dove, which comes back with an olive leaf. This indicates the period of whiteness mixed with greenness.

The final dove that was released never returns. This is symbolic of the stage of completion, in which the preliminary stages of the stone have been replaced by the final, perfected form of the red elixir, which has been multiplied and made more fruitful, or powerful. The nonreturn of the final dove after seven days was interpreted to mean that the extent of dry land had increased, or multiplied, substantially, so that the dove found its home elsewhere.

The release of the four birds supposedly took twenty-eight days, during which time the extent of earth multiplied and became fruitful. This is precisely the period of time required to complete the first process of multiplication. The text then states that Noah climbed out of the ark to make burnt offerings. This may be interpreted as taking the elixir out of the vessel (ark) and performing transmutations in the fire.

The time frames involved in the progression of the Flood thus precisely correspond to the time frames involved in the phases of the work, as described by Philalethes and others. If the ancient Hebrew tradition was actually a tradition of alchemical priests, then the idea that they would encode their secret alchemical knowledge in a mythical setting does not seem far-fetched. It is consistent with the traditional notion that the Bible encodes many secrets available only to those who have the "eyes to see" and the "ears to hear."

The Two Stone Tablets

Another important account in the Bible revolves around the Tablets of Testimony received by Moses on Mount Sinai. The two stone tablets reportedly had the words of God inscribed upon them, which conveyed the Ten Commandments. But in actual fact no one ever saw the writing on the tablets, if there was any, except Moses and his inner circle, who served to interpret the word of God for the people.

The Bible tells us that the Israelites had just come out of Egypt, where they had been kept in bondage, but that Moses had been raised by the daughter of the pharaoh. This implies that Moses had been raised in the Egyptian royal court and would have been privy to the secrets of the Egyptian royalty and priesthood.

The Egyptians commonly worshipped stones as the concretized essence of God on earth. The most famous of these stones was the mysterious *benben* stone worshipped at Heliopolis, the most ancient and sacred seat of wisdom in all of Egypt. Hellenistic authors tell us that the benben stone was fashioned from the ashes of the phoenix by means of a gum resin, which held the ashes together and allowed them to be fashioned into a stone, worshipped as a form of God.

The Hermetic texts tell us that the ancient Egyptians "made" their gods, or stone representations of the gods, by combining ordinary matter such as crushed stone with another type of material substance that was considered divine.

> The gods whose shapes are fashioned by mankind are made of both substances, that is, of the divine substance, which is purer and far nobler (than man), and the substance which is lower than man, namely, the (ordinary) material of which they are wrought.[9]

These two substances were combined to make a special type of synthetic stone, which could be molded into a pyramidal or conical shape such as the benben stone, or into any other shape such as that of a statue. According to the Hermetic texts, these stone objects or statues were viewed as being endowed with life, or consciousness, such that they emanated a spiritual presence that could profoundly affect the awareness of those who came into their proximity, by inducing visions and prophetic dreams.

> I mean statues, but statues living and conscious, filled with the breath of life, and doing many mighty works . . . by prophetic inspiration, and by dreams, and in many other ways; statues which inflict diseases and heal them, dispensing sorrow and joy according to men's merits.[10]

It was not the "form" of the stone that produced these miraculous effects. The text implies that the miraculous effects had their origin in the "divine substance" out of which the stone objects were, at least partially, made.

The idea that the ancient Egyptians possessed a secret science of stone-making has more recently been advocated by Professor Joseph Davidovits, a French expert in geopolymers. In the process of his research, Davidovits uncovered a number of texts that support his theory. In the Louvre Museum in Paris, for example, is the four-thousand-year-old Irtysen Stela, the funerary stela of Irtysen, a master craftsman of the priestly class, who lived at the end of the Old Kingdom era. The hieroglyphic inscription on the stela states that Irtysen possessed a "secret knowledge" that enabled him to fabricate stone statues, not by carving them but by casting them in molds. More specifically, it states that he used a "material mixture that hardened when cast inside molds to reproduce any kind of object or figure—a material that could not be burned in fire, nor water dilute."[11]

Certain ancient Egyptian artifacts are consistent with this notion. Below the base of the Sakkara step pyramid, the first pyramid built in Egypt by the famous architect Imhotep, some thirty thousand stone vessels were found. After examining these exquisite vessels, Professor Davidovits commented:

> These are unique and enigmatic hard stone vessels, made of slate, diorite, and basalt. Some of these materials are harder than iron. No sculptor today would even attempt to work with such material.

One wonders how they could have been carved. Their design is extremely beautiful and impossible to carve. No tool marks are found on their surfaces. They must have been cast in molds, in accordance with the indications suggested by the Irtysen Stele at the Louvre gallery.[12]

Since the 1980s, Davidovits has also advocated a theory that the stone blocks used to construct the pyramids were not carved from limestone bedrock and carried to the site, but were synthetic stones cast at the construction site itself. Although he has faced strong opposition from Egyptologists, his theory appears to be based upon sound scientific reasoning and a detailed analysis of the pyramid stones themselves.

Whether or not the Egyptians applied their secret science of stonemaking on such a grand scale remains a matter of dispute. But it is typically believed that the missing capstone of the Great Pyramid directly corresponds to the benben stone, which Hellenistic authors suggest was actually a synthetic stone made from the ashes of the phoenix. In all of the ancient myths the phoenix was linked with the pursuit of immortality, and in the medieval alchemical traditions the resurrected phoenix was directly equated with the "resurrected" forms of the metals—the elixir of immortality, or philosopher's stone, to which were ascribed two important forms: white and red.

We will discuss the white and red symbolism that pervaded the ancient Egyptian culture in more detail later. Our current interest is in the two stones that were received by Moses on top of Mount Sinai, supposedly from the hands of God himself.

The Location of Mount Sinai

The actual location of Mount Sinai is a matter of debate. In the fourth century AD, an order of Greek Christian monks, who explored the Sinai Peninsula some seventeen hundred years after the time of Moses, decided that the mountain Moses referred to as Mount Sinai corresponds to a mountain located in the southern Sinai, which has since become known as Mount Sinai. Although no archaeological evidence exists to support this notion, for the last sixteen hundred years this has been the popular belief. With the advent of modern archaeology, this old belief is beginning to wane. Today there are thirteen or fourteen different theories as to where the mountain was actually located.

Of particular interest to our discussion is a theory presented in some detail by Sir Laurence Gardner in his book *Genesis of the Grail Kings*. Gardner's theory is based upon the archaeological work of Sir Flinders Petrie, in the early twentieth century.

What the Bible does not make clear is that in Moses's time, the Sinai Peninsula was under Egyptian control. The Egyptians had used the Sinai to mine copper from malachite and other copper-based minerals, such as turquoise, for well over a thousand years prior to the time of the Exodus. As such the Sinai Peninsula had been and still was under the control of the Egyptian royalty and their appointed vassals when Moses and the Israelites made their journey across it.

Flinders Petrie, who is credited by many as being the father of

Palestinian archaeology and who was a professor at London's University College, made a proposal in the 1890s to the Egyptian Exploration Fund for an expedition into the Sinai. The articles of the fund authorized it to finance archaeological expeditions that might shed light on biblical teachings.

On this particular expedition, which actually began in 1904, Flinders Petrie was commissioned to explore southward into the Sinai to see if he could uncover any signs of the biblical Exodus. On his way south, Flinders Petrie's expedition came upon a solitary mountain rising to a height of 2,600 feet, located on a high desert plateau several hundred miles north of what was believed to be Mount Sinai at the time. To the locals this was known as Serâbît el-Khadim (the Prominence of the Khadim).

Upon climbing to the summit, the expedition discovered clear signs of human habitation. Although the site was covered with rubble deposited by wind and landslides, they could see pillars and standing stones protruding through the debris. This excited Flinders Petrie to no end, because prior to his discovery and subsequent clearing of the rubble, the site was completely unknown. Gardner cites a quote from Flinders Petrie:

> There is no other such monument which makes us regret that it is not in better preservation. The whole of it was buried, and no one had any knowledge of it until we cleared the site.

What Petrie discovered was an ancient Egyptian temple complex devoted to the goddess Hathor, dating back to the time of King Sneferu, (ca. 2600 BCE), whose immediate ancestors built the Great Pyramids. But it also became apparent that the complex had been continuously occupied and operated well into the New Kingdom, because pillars devoted to a number of New Kingdom pharaohs, such as Tuthmose III and Ramses I, were also found there. A recent photo of a portion of the ancient ruins is presented in figure 1.

Among the many artifacts found at the site were crucibles such as those used by metallurgists of the period, and stone grinding tables such as those used to grind stones and ores into powders. Petrie concluded that the temple must have had some type of metallurgical purpose, perhaps involving the copper-bearing minerals that are relatively abundant in the Sinai region.

Flinders Petrie made another intriguing discovery. Buried beneath the heavy flagstones of a storeroom he found substantial quantities of a fine white powder, which he assumed had some ritualistic or metallurgical purpose. Upon winnowing the powder to see if it contained any bone fragments, it was determined that it did not. The stash consisted entirely of an unadulterated white powder, fine as talc. Gardner reports that some of the powder was taken back to Britain for analysis, but no results were ever published, and over the years since then, the exposed stash has blown away in the desert wind.

Most of Flinders Petrie's detailed report regarding his expedition

Fig. 1. Ancient ruins devoted to the goddess Hathor and later to New Kingdom pharaohs

was withheld by the Egyptian Exploration Fund from its subscribers. The problem was that Flinders Petrie believed he had discovered the location of Mount Sinai, where Moses received the Tablets of Testimony and delivered to the people the sacred manna called "bread." Flinders Petrie's proposal that Mount Sinai was the site of an ancient Egyptian temple, active during the time of Moses, was just too radical for the administrators of the fund to accept; they didn't want to lose credibility with their subscribers.

According to the Bible, Moses himself was raised in the Egyptian royal court by the daughter of the pharaoh. This would have given him access to many important contacts throughout Egypt, with whom he likely had alliances. The complex at Mount Serâbît el-Khadim was the only major temple complex in the Sinai at the time, and Gardner speculates that Moses may have had friends (or even relatives) there who were sympathetic with his cause and would have given his band of refugees shelter and food.

The Bible tells us that Moses and the Israelites camped for an extended period at the foot of Mount Sinai, during which time Moses ascended to the summit and spent forty days praying to God for guidance, while the people below were forbidden to approach or even come close, at the threat of death.

> You must put barriers round the mountain and say, "Take care not to go up the mountain or even to touch the edge of it." Any man who touches the mountain must be put to death. No hand shall touch him; he shall be stoned or shot dead.[13]

From below, the people could see smoke rising from the summit as if from a "kiln."

> Mount Sinai was all smoking because the Lord had come down upon it in fire; the smoke went up like the smoke of a kiln.[14]

Why was this specific metallurgical analogy used? Was Moses preparing the "stones" on top of Mount Sinai using secret alchemical methods? One has to remember that it was Moses himself who wrote this account. Why did he slip into this metallurgical analogy? The official and public version is that he received the two stone tablets from God himself, who appeared to him in the form of a burning bush. But what was he really doing up there on top of the mountain? If Flinders Petrie and Gardner are correct in their opinions that Mount Sinai was actually Serâbît el-Khadim, then the smoke seen rising from the mountain may very well have been smoke from a kiln.

Was Moses working with the Egyptian priests stationed in the temple complex on the summit to produce synthetic stones, perhaps made using the mysterious white powder, which would provide a concrete representation of the "presence of God" for the people below?

The Ark of the Covenant

The people whom Moses was leading out of Egypt had lived there for some four hundred years. They may have hated the Egyptian royal families, who had cast them in bondage, but it is likely that they had adopted the Egyptian religion. Prior to Moses, there was no such thing as the "Jewish religion." It didn't exist. All that existed was Hebrew lore.

Moses invented the Jewish religion, but he had to do so with delicate gloves. He had to gradually wean the Israelites away from their adopted Egyptian religion and convert them to his new Jewish religion, which was closer to their own cultural roots. The Exodus account makes it clear that the people often revolted against his new ideas. To partially appease them, Moses allowed the Israelites to end their daily prayers with the word *amen,* which was the name of one of the most popular Egyptian gods of the time. It's rather ironic that Christian and Jewish prayers are made in the name of an Egyptian god, but that's the historical fact.

As mentioned previously, in ancient Egypt the concrete representations of the gods on earth were embodied in the form of stones or stone statues, which were believed to possess enormous spiritual power, capable of engendering visionary states of consciousness in those who came in their immediate proximity. But in Egypt, the common people were not given direct access to the gods. This was reserved for the priests alone, who hid away the stone gods in the inner sanctums of their temples, where they were kept in golden arks or boxes made of acacia wood and gold—deemed the houses of the gods. On festival and holy days, the arks containing the stone gods were draped in animal skins and cloth, taken out of the inner sanctum, and paraded through the streets by the priests and their assistants, so the people could pay homage to the gods. But the people never actually got to see the stone gods.

This was the religious practice with which the people camped at the base of Mount Sinai were familiar, and so Moses incorporated this ancient Egyptian practice into his new Jewish religion. As in Egypt, the stone tablets carried down from the mountain by Moses were never seen by the people, other than the first (and second) time he brought them down. Even then, the people saw them only from a distance. The stone tablets were quickly put into the Ark of the Covenant, which was kept in the inner sanctum of the tabernacle tent, which Moses had constructed to house the ark and its precious contents.

Only Moses and his inner circle were allowed to enter the inner sanctum, where the presence of God was made manifest, and even for them a certain degree of ritual purity was required. There are instances recalled in the Bible and various Jewish legends where those without the required spiritual purity entered into the presence of the ark and were struck dead on the spot or suffered terrible diseases—a feature also associated with the Egyptian stone gods.

This was not due to the power of the ark itself. The ark was merely the container, or house, in which the stones were kept. The presence of God was manifest by the stones and not the mere box in which they were kept. The Bible tells us that when Moses would enter the inner sanctum and come into the presence of the ark or stones, he would speak with God, and his face would be so transfigured that he had to wear a veil to hide his transfiguration from the people.

If the legends are true, then it is quite clear that these were no ordinary stones. They were none other than spiritual stones, or philosopher's stones, similar to the synthetic ones made by the Egyptians to embody the gods using both ordinary matter, such as crushed stone, and another mysterious divine substance, which imbued the stones with "life" and "consciousness," such that they formed a dimensional gateway into the other world—the mysterious world of spirit. Is it possible that these mysterious "god-stones" were made from a synthetic mixture of ordinary stone and the sacred philosopher's stone?

The Manna

The stones were not the only things kept in the ark. According to the Bible, God instructed Moses to keep an omer of manna in the ark so that future generations would have an example of the "bread" that the Lord had given them to eat while in the wilderness.

As will be discussed in more detail later, this was also a part of the ancient Egyptian religion. According to the Egyptian texts and records, a mysterious "white bread" was made by the high priests in the house of life (*per ankh*) located in Heliopolis, which the Egyptians called "On." But this was no ordinary bread. It was an alchemical elixir prepared by the Egyptian priests so that the pharaoh could become like the *shemsu-hor,* the descendants or followers of Horus. The myths hold that the shemsu-hor founded the mystery school in Heliopolis during predynastic times, and from them the race of pharaohs descended. *The Egyptian Book of the Dead* states that those who consume the white bread and red ale produced by the priests in the house of life will become forever like the followers of Horus.

> Let there be given to him (white) bread and (red) ale which have been issued in the Presence of Osiris, and he will be forever like the Followers of Horus.[15]

The book of Genesis tells us that Joseph, an ancestor of Moses and the great-grandson of Abraham, was married to the daughter of the priest of On (Heliopolis). In ancient times, the high priest of On was like the Catholic pope. The biblical notion that his daughter was married to Joseph carries huge significance: It indicates a marriage between the Egyptian and Hebrew lines of alchemical priests.

It also implies that Moses would have been quite familiar with the mysterious Egyptian "white bread" produced by the priests of On and consumed by the Egyptian royalty for the sake of spiritual power and immortality. The people who had been kept in bondage by the Egyptian royalty, on the other hand, were likely unfamiliar with this substance, which in Egypt was reserved for the royal and priestly classes. Thus, when the mysterious white bread was introduced to the Israelites they asked:

> "What is that?" because they did not know what it was. Moses said to them, "That is the bread which the Lord has given you to eat."[16]

Just prior to this disclosure, the Bible tells us:

> That evening a flock of quails flew in and settled all over the camp, and in the morning a fall of dew lay all around. When the dew was gone, there in the wilderness, fine flakes appeared, fine as hoarfrost on the ground.[17]

The traditional interpretation is that the manna was produced by a natural or divine occurrence, such that the manna just materialized out of thin air and fell on the ground, as if by magic. But the description is perfectly consistent with alchemical code language, in which the process of distillation or sublimation was often compared to the flying and settling of birds.

When a material is distilled, it is vaporized under heat. The vapors then fly up, like a flock of birds, and are collected in a receiving vessel, where they settle like a flock of birds by condensing into droplets, often compared to dew. In the event that the material is dry, such as a powder, the process is called sublimation, which was often described using the same analogy. In this case, the vapors correspond to fine particles that ascend as a smoke, and then condense in the receiving vessel as a rind, often having the appearance of fine flakes.

Hudson and his metallurgical chemists discovered that the white powder of gold can be sublimed in this manner, at a relatively low temperature. When it settles on a cold surface, it then appears in the form of white flakes, fine as hoarfrost. But gold was not the only form of ORME listed by Hudson in his patent application. The application included monatomic materials made from a number of different transition-group elements, including copper. As noted previously, copper-bearing minerals and ores are quite abundant in the Sinai. But the Sinai Peninsula has never been a major gold-producing area.

In the event that copper ores in the Sinai region contain the white powder of copper, perhaps from prehistoric volcanic activity, then it is feasible, at least in principle, that ORME copper could have been recovered by simply crushing and grinding the native copper ore to a fine powder and then subliming the resulting white powder using heat, where it would have settled or condensed in a receiving vessel, or even on the relatively cold ground, in the form of fine white flakes. The passage quoted above thus appears to be a veiled allusion to the process by which the manna was made. In fact, the stash of fine white powder found at the Egyptian temple on top of Serâbît el-Khadim may very well have been a stash of ORME copper. Was this the manna?

The idea that the manna was "made" by Moses and his inner

circle is consistent with the fact that the Bible tells us that the manna was put out for the people only six days of the week. Manna was not offered on the Sabbath, because the Sabbath was a day of rest, when no work was to be done. If the manna was being made by Moses and his craftsmen, then they would not have been allowed to work or produce any manna on that day.

It is unlikely that the manna was the true philosopher's stone. More than likely it consisted of the "seeds of copper"—the white monatomic powder of copper that could be recovered from the copper ores in the area and consumed for spiritual purposes as sacred white bread, or food for the soul. The Bible suggests that the white powder was shaped into wafers, perhaps using honey as a binding ingredient. With the advent of the Roman Catholic Church, the wafers of manna became symbolized by the hosts—the white wafers made from ordinary flour used in the holy sacrament.

The Bible tells us that the sacred "shew bread," corresponding to unleavened white wafers of manna, was made by Bezalel. He is described as a master craftsman of copper, silver, and gold. If the shew bread was made from ordinary flour, then why have a master metallurgist prepare it?

Self-Organization and Self-Decay

The Bible also tells us that the people were instructed to eat the manna on the same day they received it; otherwise; it would go bad. Why? The simple and obvious answer is that the manna must have been made from biological substances, such that it would rot in the desert heat. But in my opinion that answer is incorrect. My view is that the manna was made from inorganic substances, such as the white powder of copper. But if this is true, then how could it possibly go bad? To provide an answer, we need to take a short scientific detour.

During the 1970s, when I was working on my master's degree at an academy in Switzerland, one of the visiting professors was Ilya Prigogine, who later received the Noble Prize in Chemistry for his revolutionary theory of nonequilibrium thermodynamics. Prigogine's theory explained the mysterious process of self-organization displayed by certain systems, including living systems, whereby they can become endowed with less entropy, or increased internal order, when they are exposed to increased thermal energy.

To explain the mechanics, Prigogine used the analogy of a pan of oil, heated slowly on the stove. If the pan is heated rapidly, then the oil simply boils, resulting in a decrease in the internal order of the system. But if the pan is heated very slowly, over a period of time, then the oil will develop circulation cells, which serve to dissipate the internal heat energy, resulting in an increase in the internal order of the system.

However, when the heat is increased very slowly and continuously, at a certain point the circulation cells will no longer be able to dissipate the heat. The cells will then break down, giving rise to a chaotic state of the oil. Prigogine explained that this represents a phase transition between one state of order and the next. As the heat continues to gradually increase, at a certain point a new set of circulation cells will be formed from the chaotic state, giving rise to a new coherent and ordered state of the fluid, which is more suitable for dispersing the increased heat energy.

In this manner, the system can bootstrap itself into higher and higher states of internal order, with intervening periods of disorder, under an external source of heat. This is called self-organization. In the event that the heat is gradually reduced, the system will display a similar sequence of ordered and disordered phases as it cools down, or undergoes a process of self-decay. Prigogine received the Nobel Prize for his theory because it has applications in many fields in physics, chemistry, and biology, where systems, far from thermodynamic equilibrium, can undergo phase transitions of this type.

In metallurgical terms, the process of slowly heating a metal over a period of time and then slowly cooling it down is called "annealing."

After a metal has been annealed, it displays different properties from before.

Hudson and his chemists acquired a very expensive piece of equipment to study the properties of ORME-type materials as they were being annealed. The equipment was such that a small sample of the material could be placed in a little metal pan and slowly heated in an inert atmosphere, while simultaneously being weighed and shielded from external magnetic fields.

When they did this, they discovered to their amazement that certain ORME materials displayed anomalous and dramatic weight (or mass) changes. At certain points in the annealing process, the material would weigh several hundred percent of its starting weight, and at other times it would weigh "less than nothing," such that the recorded weight was less than the weight of the pan before the material was put into it! These dramatic results are completely anomalous. There is no theory in physics or chemistry that can be used to explain them.

But the results are consistent with Prigogine's theory of self-organization and self-decay. It appears that as the material is being annealed, or slowly heated and cooled, it goes through phases of increased internal order (less weight) and decreased internal order (more weight) in the phase transition between ordered states. But this must involve more than just a rearrangement of the particles in the sample. We are talking about changes in the force of gravity that link the material with the gravitational force of the earth. Whatever is causing the effect must be tied to the mass of the atoms out of which the material is composed—and the mass of an atom is directly related to its nucleus.

High-Spin Nuclei

About the same time that Hudson filed his patents, nuclear physicists around the world claimed to have discovered a new and previously unknown state of the atomic nucleus, called the "high-spin state."

The high-spin state of an atomic nucleus is typically produced in nuclear accelerators using bombardment techniques, and it was determined that when in a high-spin state, the otherwise spherical shape of the nucleus becomes elongated, such that it resembles the shape of an American football (deformed) or a banana (superdeformed).

> Researchers at the Lawrence Berkeley laboratory* have been finding that rapidly spinning nuclei with different masses have similar—if not exactly the same—moments of inertia. "Something is going on," said Frank F. Stephens, a physicist at the Lawrence Berkeley lab, "and for reasons we don't understand yet." A spinning nucleus results from an off-center collision between two nuclei that fuse to form a rapidly spinning, elongated body. "The deformed nucleus can take the shape of an American football, a doorknob, or possibly even a banana depending on the collision energy in the nuclei. In a typically deformed nucleus the long axis exceeds the two short axes by a factor of about 1:3. A nucleus whose long axis is about twice that of the short axis is called superdeformed."[18]

The deformed shapes of the nucleus are now beginning to be studied on the theoretical basis of the nuclear drop model, discussed previously, which compares the atomic nucleus to a superfluid drop, which can undergo deformations and still retain its integrity, like a drop of fluid with a surface tension.

Upon learning about this research, Hudson realized that the metal atoms described in the physics literature as being capable of assuming a high-spin state were the same metal atoms that can assume an ORME state. The list of such elements is given below in accordance with their appearance in the periodic table.

---

*The Ernest Orlando Lawrence Berkeley National Laboratory is a U.S. Department of Energy facility located at the University of California, Berkeley.

TABLE OF MONATOMIC ELEMENTS

8A	8A	8A	1B	2B
	Cobalt	Nickel	Copper	
Ruthenium	Rhodium	Palladium	Silver	
Osmium	Iridium	Platinum	Gold	Mercury

According to nuclear physics, not only is the atom composed of electrons orbiting around the nucleus but the nucleus itself is composed of nucleons (protons and neutrons) that orbit around the center of the nucleus. The high-spin state involves an acceleration of those nuclear orbits, such that the nucleons are spinning around inside the nucleus faster than in an ordinary atom.

Hudson thus concluded that the rearranged electron orbits of the monatomic elements must be tied to rearranged nuclear orbits, and began to tout the monatomic materials as high-spin elements. Although his claim remains largely unsubstantiated, it is consistent with the fact that an orbitally rearranged atom no longer displays the typical spectroscopic emissions of the same atom in an ordinary state.

After an electron orbital becomes excited, it gradually decays back toward its ground state in discrete steps, emitting electromagnetic radiation along the way. The possible emission spectrum for each type of atom is unique and provides a means for identifying, or assaying, the atoms inherent in a given sample of material. We know for a fact that the electron emission spectrum for the monatomic elements is different from any of the known emission spectra, hence the ORME atoms don't show up in a standard assay.

A similar type of phenomenon occurs when a nuclear orbital becomes excited. The orbit slows down in discrete steps, emitting high-energy gamma radiation. But in a high-spin or superdeformed nucleus, the spectral emissions are different from in an ordinary nucleus.

> It is in these superdeformed nuclei that curious goings-on have taken place. A spinning superdeformed nucleus slows down in discrete steps, each time emitting gamma rays, or highly energetic photons. The emissions produce a characteristic band of energy spikes all spaced equally apart. The surprise: the spectra of some different superdeformed nuclei were almost identical.[19]

Although the orbital states of the nucleons are different from the orbital states of the electrons, the two types of orbits are necessarily linked by electrostatic and electromagnetic forces within the structure of an atom. It thus seems reasonable to presume that if the electron orbits are rearranged, then the nuclear orbits must also be rearranged, and vice versa. Hence, Hudson came to the conclusion that the ORME atoms must have a high-spin nucleus, similar to that which is described in the physics literature.

This conclusion is also consistent with the results of the annealing experiments, which demonstrate changes in the mass of the atoms as they are slowly heated and cooled. This must have something to do with the changing states of the atomic nucleus during the annealing process, because the nucleus acts as the primary source of mass within an atom.

Is it possible that the superfluid nucleus of an ORME atom undergoes a process of self-organization during the annealing process, such that it bootstraps itself into higher and higher internal circulation states, similar to the way that a pan of oil bootstraps itself into higher circulation states when it is slowly heated?

Vedic myth tells us that the nectar of immortality is produced by churning the ocean of consciousness. Does the annealing process churn the superfluid nucleus of an ORME atom so that the atom becomes more potent in its spiritual effects? Do these effects then decay over time, such that an ORME atom gradually loses its spiritual potency after being taken out of the furnace?

If so, then this could account for the mysterious biblical notion that the manna had to be consumed as soon as it was received, otherwise it would go bad and decay. Here the term "bad" refers to a lack of spiritual potency, and not to a decaying biological substance.

A Firsthand Experience with ORME Gold

This understanding is consistent with anecdotal reports concerning the consumption of ORME materials. What follows was conveyed in a private conversation between myself and a highly successful biochemist (Ph.D.), who replicated and made some improvements on Hudson's wet chemistry process designed to produce the white powder of gold from pure yellow gold. Although this person wishes to remain anonymous to maintain his professional credibility, he is a friend of mine, and I can vouch for his personal and professional integrity.

According to his report, he succeeded in making about 200 milligrams of gold ORME from pure metallic gold over a period of about three months using a process similar to that revealed in this book. But there is an important difference between his improved method and Hudson's. According to Hudson's method, metallic gold must first be dissolved in aqua regia (a mixture of hydrochloric and nitric acids) and then digested in a hydrochloric-saline solution over a long period of time.

After about six weeks or so, the solution, which is ordinarily yellow or golden colored, should begin to turn green when in a concentrated state. This is the sign that the gold has turned monatomic. At this point, Hudson tells us that one should precipitate the gold from the solution in the form of a monatomic gold-hydroxide. When one precipitates the gold at this stage, however, one obtains a reddish brown powder or sludge, which then must be annealed in a tube furnace while flooding the sample with various gases to obtain the snow-white powder of pure monatomic gold.

The biochemist, on the other hand, took the process further. Rather than precipitating the gold at the first sign of greenness, he continued the digestion for a full three months, until the solution remained green whether in a concentrated state or a dilute one. When he then precipitated the gold, it came out as a snow-white gold-hydroxide, rather than a brown gold-hydroxide—a significant difference.

After annealing the material first under hydrogen and then under argon in a tube furnace, he finally obtained a chemically inert, snow-white powder. He conducted the experiment out of scientific curiosity. But, given Hudson's claims that the material induces an altered state of consciousness, he decided to ingest a tiny amount of the material immediately after it had been made. So he measured out an amount less than one milligram (1/1000th of an aspirin), placed it in an eight-ounce glass of water, and drank it. He knew that gold itself could be consumed in small quantities with no ill effects, and that this material was chemically inert anyway, so he figured this tiny amount could not possibly harm him.

There were no immediate effects. He went home, had dinner, and settled in for a quiet evening of television with his wife. But about four hours later, he began to experience dramatic changes in his awareness—changes that terrified him. He initially thought he was dying or perhaps going insane. He later explained to me that his awareness was expanding so rapidly that he did everything he could to hold on to his ordinary reality—by distracting himself with all his power. But the experience did not go away. It did not go away that night or the next day. In fact, it lasted for approximately two months!

During this time, whenever he would settle down to rest during the day or when he would lie down to go to sleep at night, his mind would begin to expand into places he had never dreamed of—and without any knowledge of the higher spiritual planes, the experience terrified him. He imagined that he had permanently damaged his nervous system. We recall that all of the ancient traditions associated the alchemical elixirs with the expansion of consciousness, which they described as a form of ascension.

He also noticed certain physical effects. He first began to experience heat flashes within his body. Within three days of taking the material, his body also broke out in red spots resembling hives. He went to a doctor, who performed all kinds of tests, but the tests all came back negative. The diagnosis was that he was perfectly healthy.

Upon discussing his experience with me later, he made the offhand comment that he did not sleep a wink during the entire two-month period! When I suggested that he must have been exhausted, he told me that he had felt just the opposite. He felt refreshed and alert during the day and also experienced various extrasensory perceptions—such as knowing who was calling when the phone rang, and knowing when someone had arrived outside at his place of work—even though he could neither see nor hear them arrive. When he lay down to go to sleep at night, he explained he would go to a place where "time and space do not exist," and would remain awake in that state, thinking no thoughts, until morning.

It turns out that this "sleeplessness" is a common characteristic of the early stages of spiritual enlightenment. In the Vedic tradition, this was called the "sleepless state." One who becomes enlightened was thus said to have conquered sleep. The body goes to sleep and gets a deep state of rest, but the consciousness remains awake, without thinking any thoughts or having dreams. The same type of experience is described in the Hermetic texts.

> My bodily sleep had come to be sober wakefulness of soul; and the closing of my eyes true vision; and my silence pregnant with good.[20]

When my biochemist friend told me about his experience, it was six months after he had first ingested the gold ORME. He explained that the effect gradually wore off. But he dared not take any more—it was simply too powerful. Perhaps not only is the substance too powerful, but the typical human is not vibrationally attuned enough to receive it. If one became more highly attuned, such as through meditation, for example, one probably could assimilate the substance a little more easily.

So I asked him to send some to me to test for myself. Upon receiving the material and confirming that it was indeed ORME, several friends and I ingested small quantities—but noticed no effects. When I reported this to him, he decided to test it again himself, and he also noticed no effects.

We eventually arrived at the conclusion that gold ORME appears to lose its potency over time. It displays a number of unusual properties when it is first taken out of the annealing furnace, but it apparently loses those properties over time. It is still in an ORME state but it ceases to produce any notable subjective effects.

This leads to the speculation that when the ORME materials are annealed, they are elevated to a higher spin state by a process of self-organization, which gradually decays back toward a ground state after being taken out of the furnace. If the manna consisted of copper ORME, it would likely display a similar type of decay. Hence, the people were told to eat it the same day it was created.

Nourishment for the Body and Soul

The Bible also tells us that the people were instructed to take an omer of manna per person each day. An omer is a volumetric measure now set equal to the volume of 43.2 average eggs, which is a rather large quantity. Whether an omer was this large in biblical times is a matter of debate, but in all likelihood an omer was not a tiny amount.

No one really knows how many Israelites came with Moses out of Egypt, but the biblical accounts suggest that it was more than just a few, probably thousands. This means that thousands of omers of copper ORME had to be produced every day, six days a week! Even given the size of the temple complex on top of Serâbît el-Khadim, this would have been a tall order to fill.

The more likely scenario is that Moses and his inner circle mixed a small quantity of the white powder of copper with a much larger quantity of ordinary white flour, so that the people actually made unleavened bread with the mystery material. This would have served to nourish both their bodies and their souls.

In effect, the bread was spiked with the white powder of copper. Whereas the bread nourished their bodies, the white copper nourished their souls. If the white copper induced spiritual experiences anything like those recounted by my biochemist friend, then no doubt the people would have wondered "What is that?" In effect, Moses told them, "This is holy bread."

But the white powder of copper and the white powder of gold are both a far cry from the true philosopher's stone. I shudder to think of the spiritual potency of the final forms of the true elixir. According to the alchemical tradition in India, the final elixirs are not something to be taken lightly or for recreational purposes. Those who were to take the elixirs were required to go through an arduous process of both spiritual and bodily purification over a long period of time before they were ready for the final elixirs. This was called *kshetrikarana*—"making (oneself master of) the field."[21] It involved a regimen of special diets, breathing exercises, emetics, hot oil baths, et cetera.

Apparently the people whom Moses led out of the Sinai were not quite ready for the true elixirs, and so they were given its lesser form, corresponding to fresh copper ORME. Moses and his inner circle, on the other hand, may have used the true elixirs for their own spiritual purposes, and the mysterious and extremely powerful stones kept in the ark were also likely made from them.

Unfortunately, the Ark of the Covenant and the mysterious stones that it contained have been lost. The omer of manna placed within the ark to provide a record of the bread that the people ate has been lost along with it. The third thing kept in the ark was the budding rod of Aaron, the brother of Moses, who was consecrated as a high priest of the new Jewish religion. This may very well have been a hollow golden rod filled with the true elixir and thus assigned magical and life-giving (budding) properties, as though it were a magic wand or staff.

This is all historical speculation, of course, based upon my perspective, which has a strong alchemical slant. But it makes sense and may even have a scientific basis. Whatever the actual historical facts might have been, it seems apparent that the Jews and their ancestors possessed knowledge of alchemy that dates back at least to the time of Moses. If the books of Moses, which purport to record the history of the biblical patriarchs, are taken for their hidden alchemical meanings, then it can be argued that this knowledge extends back much farther, to the time of the Garden of Eden itself.

FOUR

Egyptian Alchemy

Egyptian Land Symbolism

Pseudo-Democritus, one of the early commentators on the Hellenistic practice of alchemy, which emerged in Alexandrine Egypt, tells us:

> It was the law of the Egyptians that nobody must divulge these things in writing.[1]

He was likely talking about old Egyptians laws, which predated the advent of the Ptolemies, when Alexander the Great conquered Egypt in 332 BCE. Almost two thousand years later, R. A. Schwaller de Lubicz, an ardent Egyptologist who spent twenty years living in Egypt studying the ancient monuments, expressed a similar opinion.

> The Ancients never "popularized" anything; to the uninitiated they provided only the minimal *useful* teaching. The explanation, the philosophy, the secret connection between myth and the sciences were the prerogative of a handful of specially instructed men. Did not Pythagoras wait twenty years before being admitted into the Temple? Did he not, in his own teaching, impose

> silence on pain of death? Therefore, this teaching was not written down.[2]

Schwaller de Lubicz believed that many of the Egyptian monuments and temples were literally "sermons in stone," which served to encode the wisdom of the Egyptians. The magnificent architecture of the pyramids and temples may have been on public display, but the inner sanctums of those structures and the secret wisdom they embodied were the prerogative of the elite classes alone.

Unlike the Jews, who conveyed their knowledge of alchemy using a secret language, the Egyptians conveyed their knowledge using a secret symbolism, which was tied to the land and the monuments of stone erected upon it. If we want to decipher the alchemical wisdom of the Egyptians, we have to decipher the land itself.

The Hermetic texts tell us that the land of Egypt was originally designed to be an image of heaven.

> Do you not know . . . that Egypt is an image of heaven, or, to speak more exactly, in Egypt all the operations of the powers which rule and work in heaven have been transferred to the earth below?[3]

This sentiment is echoed in the *Edfu Temple Texts,* the hieroglyphic texts inscribed on the walls of the Edfu Temple. They tell us that during the predynastic period known as *zep tepi* ("first time"), a mysterious group of "builder gods," also described as "seven sages," walked the Nile Valley and surveyed the land, marking the sites where monuments and temples were to be built. The purpose of this survey was to lay out the plans for a future kingdom that would resemble the homeland of the gods—or a kingdom of heaven on earth.

This implies that the organization of the land and the various symbols and myths tied to the land were purposefully designed to convey secret meanings—which predate the earliest historical dynasties. Some of those meanings were profoundly alchemical.

The Myth of Osiris

The central and defining myth of the land is recorded in the myth of Osiris. According to this myth, Osiris was the first god-king of Egypt, who arrived on the scene long before the first historical dynasty was founded or the first Egyptian temple was built. When Osiris arrived in Egypt, the people were living as uncultured naked cannibals, killing and consuming one another.

Whether or not this myth is rooted in historical events is immaterial for the purpose of our discussion. The symbolism is such that when Osiris arrived upon the scene he inherited a land of death, a land of spiritual darkness, where he was the only ray of light. The original kingdom of Osiris was thus called Khemi—the Black Land. It was upon this black land that the kingdom of heaven, the kingdom of eternal life, was to be built.

The myth tells us that to begin this process, Osiris first had to educate the natives in the ways of the gods. He taught them the rudiments of agriculture, language, and how to worship the gods. In the process, Osiris became their king, and his wife and half sister, Isis, became their queen. As a descendant of the sun god Ra, Osiris established the first solar dynasty in the land of Egypt. He was the solar king and Isis was his lunar queen. But they were not just secular rulers; they were spiritual rulers—for they themselves were worshipped as gods.

Osiris was the philosophic king and Isis the philosophic queen. Their royal marriage was designed to give rise to a paradisiacal kingdom—an immortal kingdom of heaven on earth. In an alchemical context, they represent the philosophic gold (the sun) and the philosophic mercury (the moon), whose alchemical marriage is designed to give rise to the stone of paradise—the elixir of immortality.

But before the kingdom of paradise could be obtained, the king and the queen had to pass through the gate of blackness and be consumed by death. The sun (Osiris) and the moon (Isis) had to pass through the eclipse and survive the purgatory of the black land before their natures could be truly renovated and their marriage consummated. It is only then that the land would become illumined by the light of paradise and the kingdom rendered immortal. This, too, has a deep alchemical parallel. Consider the following passage from Philalethes:

> But before the renovation of these Natures, they must in the first place pass through the Eclipse, both of the Sun (gold) and Moon (mercury) and the darkness of Purgatory, which is the Gate of Blackness, and after that they shall be renovated with the light of Paradise. This Allegorically is called Death.[4]

Philalethes is talking about the phase of blackness through which, after their initial marriage, the philosophic gold and philosophic mercury must pass and be reduced to a state of blackness—a fine black powder, or black earth. This was called the Gate of Blackness. The king and queen must pass through this gate, that is, the gate of death, before their marriage is fully consummated and the divine child—the elixir of immortality—is born.

In the Egyptian myth, the divine child is represented by Horus, the firstborn son of the king Osiris and the queen Isis. The myth tells us that Horus was conceived by Isis from the dead body of Osiris. In order for the child to be born, Osiris had to die. In order for the elixir to be born, the philosophic gold has to die; it has to be reduced to black ashes. But from those ashes, the exalted gold—the true philosopher's stone—is born with the assistance of the philosophic mercury. From the dead body of Osiris, his son Horus was born, with the assistance of Isis, the philosophic queen. The alchemical symbolism should be clear. But the story doesn't end here.

The White and Red Kingdoms

The myth tells us that with the death of Osiris, the land of Egypt became usurped by his brother, Set, who was instrumental in his death. Set established a new kingdom on the black land, which can be called the White Kingdom, because it was ruled by the white crown—the *hedjet.*

In an alchemical context, this represents the phase of whiteness that follows the phase of blackness. This is the phase when the elixir is first born as the Medicine of the First Order—that is, the white elixir, which serves to nourish the body. Although the elixir is conceived in the phase of blackness, it is actually born in the phase of whiteness. Although Horus was conceived from the dead body of Osiris, he was actually born when the white crown ruled the land.

The White Kingdom was the first kingdom to be resurrected on the original black land. But actually it was neither a spiritual kingdom nor a kingdom of heaven. It was a secular kingdom, a kingdom of earth. The white elixir is the first form of the elixir to be resurrected from the phase of blackness. It is really an elixir not of *im*mortality but of *mor*-tality; it serves to nourish the body rather than the soul. Once again, the alchemical parallel should be clear.

According to the myth, Horus and Isis eventually, through magical means, were able to resurrect Osiris from death. But Osiris was no longer interested in worldly affairs. He abdicated his worldly rule to his son Horus, and then ascended the stairway to the sky to obtain immortality in the bosom of the infinite, where he became known as the Lord of Immortality.

Horus then established the second kingdom on the land. It can be called the Red Kingdom, because it was ruled by the red crown—the *deshret.* This was a true spiritual kingdom, a kingdom of heaven. In an alchemical context, the Red Kingdom represents the phase of redness, when the true elixir of immortality is obtained.

The Red Kingdom, which came last, was viewed as being better and more honorable that the White Kingdom. Similarly, the red elixir, which comes last, was viewed as being better and more honorable than the white elixir. According to the sages, one cannot obtain the red until one first obtains the white. But before either the white or the red is obtained, the phase of blackness must be endured.

> That which is last is better and more honorable than that which is first. The (black) substance must first become white, and then red; it cannot become red unless it has first become white. Hence Simon the Sage says: "Know that unless you first make the Stone white, you cannot make it red."[5]

Once again, the parallel should be clear. Although one might imagine that the European alchemists drew their alchemical symbolism from the land symbolism of Egypt, this cannot be. When the alchemists wrote their treatises, Egypt was a largely forgotten land, a faint memory recorded in the Bible and various classical texts, about which little was known. It was not until the time of Napoleon (nineteenth century) that the Rosetta stone was found and Egyptology began to take shape. It was only then that the myths, legends, monuments, and maps of Egypt began to be studied in earnest by European scholars.

The European alchemists, however, claimed that they had inherited their knowledge from a much more ancient source, that their knowledge had been passed down through a secret tradition since time immemorial. The principal source of that tradition was Egypt, whose ancient name Khemi is believed by many to be the origin of the word *alchemy.* As such, alchemy can be viewed as the art and science of the Black Land—the land upon which the White and Red Kingdoms were first erected thousands of years ago. But perhaps it was also the land in which the white and red elixirs were first obtained thousands of years ago.

This presents a new alchemical interpretation of Egyptian land symbolism, which you won't find in any book on Egyptology—primarily because the vast majority of Egyptologists have little, if any, understanding of alchemy. If my interpretation is correct, this places alchemy at the very heart and center of the ancient Egyptian tradition.

Given our alchemical interpretation of the secret language of the Bible, the same thing can be said about the ancient Jewish tradition. We will soon see that the same thing can be said about the ancient Vedic tradition. This opens a whole new chapter in our understanding of ancient history—a chapter that has remained hidden for thousands of years.

Eating the White and Red Crowns

The reference to alchemy as the Royal Art goes back to the earliest periods of Egypt, when the land was divided into two kingdoms. The White Kingdom was ruled by the white crown, known as the hedjet, and the Red Kingdom was ruled by the red crown, known as the deshret. But according to Egyptian records, these were more than just crowns. They contained the charms of the gods, which could be eaten for the sake of immortality.

The earliest-known records of the religious and mythical teachings of Old Kingdom Egypt, the Pyramid Texts, date back to around 2500 BCE. These texts consist of hieroglyphic writings found engraved on the walls of the sarcophagus chambers and antechambers of ten different pyramids scattered around Egypt. The oldest and most complete such set of texts was found in the pyramid of Unas, the last king of the fifth dynasty, located in Sakkara.

Of particular interest to our current discussion is a hymn inscribed on the east gable of the antechamber to the tomb, which has become known as the Cannibal Hymn of King Unas. In this highly symbolic hymn, Unas is compared to a god who consumes the gods, as well as the symbols and charms of the gods. He is also described as having eaten the "inward parts" of the red and white crowns.

> Unas hath eaten the red crown, and he hath swallowed the white crown; the food of Unas is the inward parts, and his meat is those who live upon magical charms in their hearts. Behold, Unas eateth of that which the red crown sendeth forth, he increaseth, and the magical charms of the gods are in his belly; that which belongeth to him is not turned back from him. Unas hath eaten the whole of the knowledge of every god, and the period of his life is eternity, and the duration of his existence is everlastingness.

Throughout history, the crowns of kings and queens have been made of gold, often embellished with precious stones. There is a reason for this. In ancient times, gold and the precious stones were deemed to possess spiritual power. By wearing gold and precious stones upon the head, the awareness and spiritual power of the ruler was thus believed to be enhanced and increased.

In both the Egyptian and early Hebrew traditions, gold was also used to line the sacred boxes or arks that were viewed as the houses of the stone gods. In his popular book *Fingerprints of the Gods,* Graham Hancock cites an ancient Egyptian legend regarding the golden box of Ra, the Egyptian sun god:

> One particularly striking tradition speaks of a "golden box" in which Ra deposited a number of objects . . . A powerful and dangerous talisman, this box, together with its bizarre contents, remained enclosed in a fortress on the "eastern frontier" of Egypt until a great many years after Ra's ascent to heaven. When Geb came to power he ordered that it should be brought to him and unsealed in his presence. In the instant that the box was opened a bolt of fire (described as the "breath of the divine serpent") ushered from it, struck dead all Geb's companions, and gravely burned the god-king himself.[6]

There are numerous accounts in both the Bible and Jewish lore that describe the potent power of the golden box called the ark, which, like the golden box of Ra, held mysterious contents and could strike dead those in its presence with a bolt of fiery energy, or seriously injure them, inducing boils and sores upon their bodies. In Egyptian legend, similar accounts are described with respect to the red crown, which was considered an object of potent magic, dreaded and feared, and compared to a fiery serpent. In Utterance 221 of the Pyramid Texts we have the king's prayer:

> Ho crown of Lower Egypt! Ho Red Crown. Ho Great Crown! Ho Crown great of magic! Ho Fiery Serpent! Grant that the dread of me be like the dread of you; grant that the fear of me be like the fear of you . . .

Is it possible that the white and red crowns were designed as hollow golden receptacles, to be worn on the head, whose inward parts were filled with the white and red elixirs—the resurrected forms of philosophic gold? If so, then the inward parts could be eaten for the sake of immortality, as described in the Cannibal Hymn.

This goes back to the notion, discussed in the introduction, that spiritualized forms of the metals were used to uphold the worldly and spiritual powers of the elite ruling classes in the earliest civilizations on earth. The implication is that the rulers not only wore the elixirs on their heads in the form of golden vessels, or crowns, which conferred worldly power, but also ate the elixirs stored in the crowns to obtain great spiritual power.

The notion that the ancients wore the elixirs on their bodies can also be found in the siddha tradition of Indian alchemy. The alchemical siddhas ("perfected ones") smeared the white elixir all over their bodies to awaken their bodily powers, and they placed the red elixir as a tilak (red dot) over their spiritual third eye to awaken their spiritual powers.

In this tradition, the white elixir was compared to the semen of Shiva, the masculine form of God, while the red elixir was compared to the menstrual blood of Shakti, the feminine form of God. By wearing the elixirs on their bodies, the perfected ones became "reborn" as embodiments of Shiva-Shakti—or embodiments of God on earth. The Egyptian pharaohs were revered in the same way. They too were viewed as embodiments of God on earth—because they wore the white and red crowns and ate their contents.

White Bread and Red Ale

The myth of Osiris goes on to tell us that eventually Horus subdued Set and united the two kingdoms into one, called the United Kingdom. He also united the two crowns into one, called the double crown—the *pschent.* All the pharaohs of the historical dynasties followed the archetype of Horus.

As long as a pharaoh wore the double crown (red and white) on his head and ruled the united land of Egypt, he was viewed as an embodiment of Horus. But when a pharaoh either abdicated the crown to his son or died, and thus set out to ascend the stairway to the sky to attain final immortality in the bosom of the infinite, he was viewed as an embodiment of Osiris, the Lord of Immortality.

In order to complete his long spiritual journey to attain immortality, a pharaoh required sustenance. The sacred sustenance used to support the life of the pharaoh while on the path of immortality was called white bread and red ale. These were the food and drink of the gods.

The white bread and red ale were sacramental substances produced by the high priests in the house of life (per ankh) at Heliopolis, which the Egyptians called On. This was also the place where the earliest renditions of the Egyptian Book of the Dead were composed. Heliopolis, or On, was to the Egyptians what Jerusalem is to the Jews and Mecca is to the Muslims.[7] It was the place where "divine words" of the gods were heard and recorded: "When a message comes from heaven, it is heard in Heliopolis."[8] It was also the place where the medical papyri, sacred elixirs, mathematical problems, instructional writings, and so forth were prepared by the priests under the divine patronage of Thoth, the Egyptian wisdom god.

The Heliopolitan priests were also the principal custodians of the sacred benben stone, which was worshipped in Heliopolis as the "divine mound" that emerged from the watery abyss in the very beginning. Believed to have been shaped like the capstone of the pyramids, the benben symbolized the summit of Egyptian wisdom and was conceived as the crystallization of the sun god Ra himself.

The benben stone was also deeply associated with the divine bird called the *bennu* bird, the "ascending one," which may be understood as the Egyptian phoenix. The pharaohs who were about to depart on their long journey by ascending the stairway to the sky were also described as "ascending ones."

In order to prepare for their ascension through the heavens, the ascending ones ate the white bread and drank the red ale prepared by the Heliopolitan priests as a type of spiritual food. The ritual of the modern Catholic Mass is an echo of this ancient practice. As in ancient Egypt, the Holy Mass involves eating white bread and drinking red wine in a ritual of spiritual transubstantiation.

Although Egyptologists insist that the white bread and red ale were nothing more than cakes prepared from white emmer and beer prepared from red barley, the symbolism surrounding these mysterious substances may merit a deeper investigation.

As noted earlier, the ancient alchemical traditions used vegetable or plant allegories to hide their secret metallurgical lore. Is it possible that the Egyptian white bread and red ale were actually the white and red elixirs, prepared from the seeds of metals rather than the seeds (grains) of plants?

The Heliopolitan wisdom school was said to have been founded by the *shemsu-hor,* literally "those who follow the path of Horus." This was also known as the "Horian way," or the "Path of Ra."[9] Horus was symbolically associated with the Udjat (Whole One), otherwise known as the all-seeing "Eye of Horus" (see figure 2).

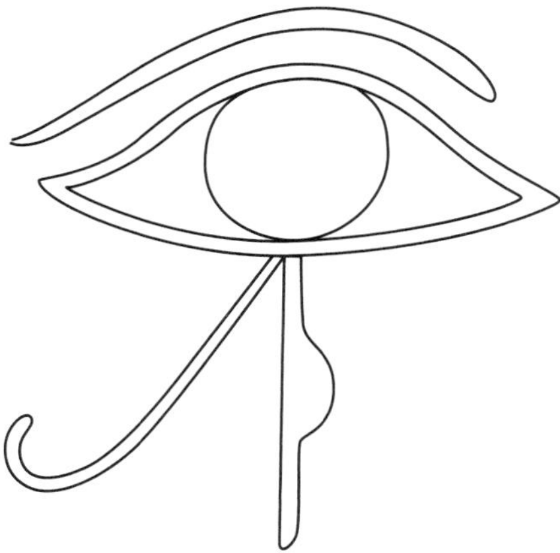

Fig. 2. The Udjat

In general, the Udjat represents the divine healing power of the gods. It signifies health, wholeness, and spiritual vision. Its function is clearly depicted in the ancient myth of Osiris, in which Horus is said to have used the mysterious power of the Udjat to resurrect and make complete his father Osiris.[10] After his resurrection, Osiris ascended the stairway to the sky to attain eternal life among the gods.

It turns out that the ancient Egyptian texts spell out a specific connection between the white bread and red ale and the Eye of Horus. For example, in the Papyrus of Ani in the Egyptian Book of the Dead, one passage describes the spiritual transformation of Ani as follows:

> Proceed, behold, you are announced (to the gods). Thy cakes [of white emmer] shall come from the Udjat (Eye of Horus), thy ale [of red barley] shall come from the Udjat. What goes forth at the voice for you upon the earth is the Udjat.[11]

At the Nefertum Chapel of Sety I at Abydos, the walls are illustrated with various scenes that are accompanied by hieroglyphic inscriptions. These inscriptions provide a direct link among the white bread, the Eye of Horus, and the sacred benben stone, as well as what is in heaven and on earth.

> I am Thoth and I appease you with the Eye-of-Horus, having brought you your meal of what is in heaven, and what is on earth. Your meal is the meal of Horus [the red ale]. Your meal is the meal of Seth [the white bread]. You have satisfied Horus with his eye [that is, the source of the red drop or elixir, resembling blood]. You have satisfied Seth with his testicles [that is, the source of the white elixir, resembling semen]. What you have sought is brought for you. What you have requested is brought for you. You have counted it in libations of wine [red ale]. I am Thoth who brings you the bright Eye-of-Horus in its name of white bread, that you might become erect through it in its name of benben.[12]

The connections here are tantalizing. The meal of Horus seems to refer to the meal of "what is in heaven," while the meal of Set appears to refer to the meal of "what is on earth." Given the fact that the kingdom of Horus was ruled by the red crown and the kingdom of Set was ruled by the white crown, these two "meals" are likely veiled references to the red elixir contained in the red crown, which gives spiritual immortality, and the white elixir contained in the white crown, which gives bodily health. In addition to being worn on the head by means of the two crowns, apparently the two elixirs were also prepared into cakes of white bread (the food of the gods) and libations of red ale (the drink of the gods) by the Heliopolitan priests.

The implication is that the grains of white emmer, from which the white bread was made, likely consisted of "grains" of the white stone. Similarly, the grains of red barley, from which the red ale was made, likely consisted of "grains" of the red stone. We note that the use of the term *grain* as a measure of weight still exists. One grain is equal to .0647 gram. Were the terms *white emmer* and *red barley* actually code words designed to hide the alchemical secrets of the Egyptian priests?

As discussed earlier, the European alchemists believed that the red elixir could be suspended in any liquid, such as water or alcohol, to form a liquid drink that had the color of red wine. In a more dilute form the liquid could assume a golden color resembling the color of beer or ale.

The red ale could have been a suspension of the red elixir in water. In this case it would represent the water of the gods—the same water carried by Aquarius in his pot. But it could also have been a suspension in alcohol—an actual red ale made from red barley. In this form, no one would know the difference between ordinary red ale and the sacred red ale, except the priests who made it and the pharaohs who drank it.

The same thing can be argued about the white bread. It may very well have been an actual white bread made from white barley, which was simply laced with the white elixir. Again, no one would know the difference between ordinary white bread and sacred white bread, except the priests who made it and the pharaohs who ate it.

Any servants who saw a king eating the sacred white bread and drinking the sacred red ale would notice nothing other than a man enjoying a meal, similar to that enjoyed by the common people of the time, who ate ordinary white bread and drank ordinary red ale. As a result, the secrets of the elite ruling classes would be preserved and the common people would be none the wiser. What an ingenious facade!

Libations of Red Ale

The bread cakes commonly consumed by the Egyptian people of the time were not shaped like ordinary loaves of bread. They were shaped into conical loaves resembling the benben stone, the proverbial capstone of the pyramids. There was thus a deep connection between the pyramids, or "Houses of Eternity," and the white bread that was prepared in the "House of Life." This is made explicit by the use of the hieroglyphic symbol of the white bread to indicate the gift of life. In

Fig. 3. "Given Life"

fact, the hieroglyph of the *ankh,* the symbol of eternal life, and that of the pyramidal loaf of bread are synonymous symbols, both of which indicate the gift of life (figure 3).

The symbol of the white bread was also used in the hieroglyph that meant "peace, contentment, and offering." It was represented by a cup that contained the sacred bread placed on a reed mat. This constituted the word *hotep,* which can be found as an inscription over virtually every tomb in ancient Egypt (figure 4).

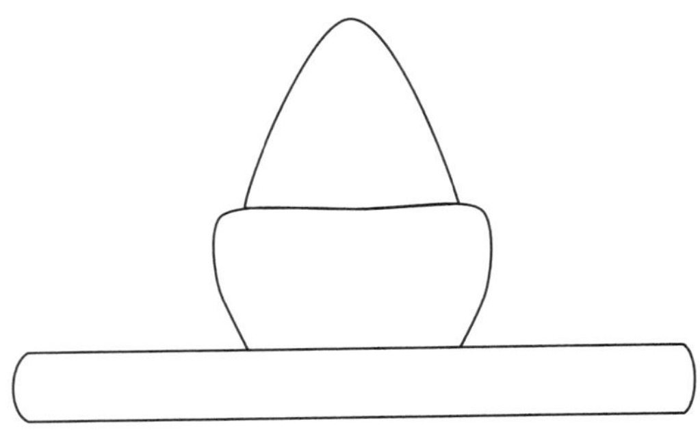

Fig. 4. Hotep
"Peace, Contentment, and Offering"

Imhotep was known as the architect of the first pyramid and the father of Egyptian medicine. As such, he would have been the master of arcane elixirs. Is it a coincidence that his name contains an image of the white bread? Clearly, something is going on here that is hidden behind the scenes.

In the Papyrus of Ani, there are a number of colored illustrations depicting various "offerings" that are being presented to the gods. More specifically, the first two illustrations depict Ani and his wife making offerings at an altar. The altar is piled high with various food substances, but on top of the pile are a number of conically shaped objects, colored white with red peaks, resembling red capstones. In the second illustration, "rays" are drawn around these conical objects, as though they are emitting some sort of spiritual radiance.

Egyptologists believe that these conical objects were mounds of congealed fat or grease, and they may very well have been. But their shape clearly suggests that they were meant to symbolize pyramidal-shaped loaves of white bread. Furthermore, the red peaks on the objects appear to indicate that they were anointed with libations of red ale, which was poured on top. This reminds us of the white Catholic wafer (the body of Christ), which is often dipped in red wine (the blood of Christ) before it is placed on the tongue of the parishioner.

Even if the objects were made of white fat, rather than white bread, they still could have been laced with the white elixir, and the red ale poured on top could have been laced with the red elixir. In the Indian tradition of alchemy, a suspension of the elixirs in oil was deemed a highly efficacious means to deliver the elixirs to the cells of the body, which were penetrated by the oils. Moreover, oils, such as ghee, or clarified butter, were often used as offerings in sacrificial rites to the gods.

This symbolism is also encoded in the Egyptian creation myths. According to the Heliopolitan tradition, the body of the sun god Ra first emerged from the watery abyss in the form of a sacred mound, represented by the benben stone. This is believed to have been a white pyramidal-shaped stone worshipped in Heliopolis. The myth tells us that once the mound emerged, the bennu bird, which represents the soul of Ra, took its perch upon the mound, as the first living creature, whose cry gave rise to all that exists.

Hieroglyphic depictions of the bennu bird most closely resemble the purple heron (*Ardea purpurea*), a migratory bird, whose name comes from its beautiful purple plumage. The purple heron still migrates through Egypt in spring and autumn, with some wintering in the marshes of the Nile Delta.

Fig. 5. The Bennu Bird

Fig. 6. The Purple Heron

The purple color of the bennu bird can also be surmised from the fact that the Egyptian word *bennu* also signifies the date palm tree, whose immature fruits are purple. In the Hellenistic era, the bennu bird was identified with the phoenix. The Greek word for "purple" is *phoeno* and the Greek word for "red" is *phoinós,* both of which are tied to the etymological derivation of the word *phoenix.*

As discussed previously, the European alchemists claimed that the final red elixir is not a bright red but a dark red, resembling congealed blood. As such, its color borders on purple. Whereas the white elixir served as food for the body, the red or purple elixir served as food for the soul, enabling the soul to ascend the stairway to the sky, like a bird, and attain immortality.

The idea that libations of red ale were poured upon the mound of white bread is thus consistent with the Egyptian creation myth, which has the purple bennu bird settling on the white bennu stone as if on a perch.

By anointing the conical loaf of white bread with red ale, the white body and red spirit become united as one, and the white body is thereby stabilized, or "made erect in its name of benben." This is also similar to the symbology of the double crown, which combines the white and red crowns into one.

As far as monumental architecture goes, the same symbology was probably reflected by the form of the Great Pyramid, whose white limestone body was likely crowned in ancient times by a red capstone, the spirit or soul of the pyramid, now missing.*[13]

The Inverted Form of Gold

Both the benben stone and the bennu bird are linked by the phoneme *ben*. Both names, *benben* and *bennu,* are thought to come from the Egyptian verb *weben,* which means "to rise in brilliance." The Egyptian word for yellow gold is *neb,* which is just the inverse of *ben*. Is this meant to provide a clue as to the true nature of the white and red elixirs?

In Hebrew, the phoneme *ben* means "son of." The European alchemists often compared the elixir to the divine child or son, born of the alchemical marriage between gold (the king) and mercury (the queen). In this sense, the elixir may be compared to the "son of gold," which surpasses its father in spiritual potency and brilliance. Mixing languages, the "son of gold" can be expressed as *ben neb,* where *ben* is Hebrew for "son of" and *neb* is Egyptian for "gold." The European alchemists

*At least one Egyptologist, William Fix, claimed to have discovered conclusive evidence that at least part of the exterior of the Great Pyramid was painted red.

claimed that the elixir was obtained by inverting the elements, such that the spiritual potential hidden inside the metals, and particularly inside gold, comes out in plain sight.

> Hence the Sages say: "Invert the elements, and you will find what you seek."[14]

If the Egyptians shared this view, then it would have been natural, given the symbolic nature of their minds, to encode this secret principle by the inverse relations between the phonemes *ben* and *neb.* In this case the Egyptian phoneme *ben* would indicate an inverted form of gold (*neb*), produced by alchemical means, such that it could be applied to the white benben stone as well as the purple bennu bird, which were mythological equivalents of the white and red elixirs.

Unfortunately, other than the Hellenistic texts, we do not have any ancient Egyptian texts that specifically describe the alchemical procedures used during the Old Kingdom. All we have are innuendo and clues provided by the symbols used in Egyptian myths and legends. But if one is capable of reading between the lines, it should be apparent that many of these symbols, myths, and legends are deeply alchemical in nature. This suggests that the practice of alchemy was with the Egyptians from the very beginning—as it was with the Jews. In the next chapter, we will discover that the same practice was also with the Indian and Chinese sages from the very beginning.

FIVE
Eastern Alchemy

Alchemical Wizards of the East

It can be reasonably argued that the Western tradition of alchemy, which flourished in the Middle East and Europe during the medieval period, had its origins in the Hebrew and Egyptian traditions. But there was also an Eastern tradition of alchemy, with origins in India and China, thousands of miles to the east.

It turns out that both alchemical traditions, Eastern and Western, believed the same theory, used the same materials, and employed the same practices to pursue the same goals. Moreover, the Eastern tradition is just as old as the Western, going back many thousands of years. How the theory and practice of alchemy became spread all over the ancient world at the very dawn of civilization remains a profound mystery, one that cannot be answered by current theories of cultural dissemination. My focus here, however, is on the substance of the practice and not on how it spread.

The East is renowned for its elaborate methods of spiritual development, involving various systems of physical, breath, and mental exercises. When one mentions meditative practices designed to yield spiritual enlightenment, one thinks of the East, where there are rich and diverse meditative traditions going back thousands of years. The histories and legends of the region are also filled with fabulous stories of enlightened masters endowed with miraculous powers who lived in hidden mountain caves or remote forest hermitages.

Moreover, the region is well known for two of the richest traditions of herbal medicine on our planet—the traditions of Chinese and Ayurvedic medicine, both of which utilize vast pharmacopeias of herbal substances. What is not so widely known is that there were also deep and ancient traditions of metallurgical alchemy in the region, which go back thousands of years.

In the Taoist tradition of China, the meditative process, which includes breath work and mental control over the subtle forces of *chi* in the body, was called the internal practice (*neidan*), while the consumption and use of alchemical elixirs was called the external practice (*weidan*). Both practices appear to have been present in the earliest periods of Chinese culture. However, around the fourth century AD, the emphasis began to shift toward the internal practice. Whether this was brought about by an increasing number of elixir poisonings or by the influence of Buddhism is unknown.

The *Baopu-zi nei pian* (Inner Chapters of the Book of the Master Who Embraces Simplicity), written by Ge Hong (ca. AD 283–343), provides insight into the typical viewpoints of Chinese alchemy. At the beginning of his treatise, Ge Hong rejects the view that only herbal drugs are beneficial for health and the prolongation of life. In the fourth chapter, he states that elixirs made from minerals and metallic substances are much more useful than the herbal ones. He claims that the herbal drugs are weak and strong heat destroys them, but that minerals and metals are strong and stable.[1] He then declares that the common or worldly people (*shi ren*) are ignorant of "such things as the nature of the cinnabar and so, it is not surprising that they do not believe in such subtle things as the way of immortality."[2]

In an interesting passage, Ge Hong writes that the common people prefer to depend upon magical, superstitious, or religious methods of healing. They do not believe in the art of the famous physicians (alchemists) but rely instead on shamans and sorcerers. As a result, it is natural that they do not believe that by eating the golden and cinnabar elixirs, immortality can be obtained. Thus, for Ge Hong, alchemy and the "arts of immortals" are not of a supernatural or religious nature; they are "positive" and "scientific" in the same way as are medicine and pharmacology.[3] Given the fact that this treatise was written in the third century AD, it indicates a deep and ancient history of alchemy that stretches back into earliest periods of Chinese culture, largely shrouded in the mists of time.

An in-depth study of the alchemical tradition of India is presented by David Gordon White in his book *The Alchemical Body*. White focuses primarily on the siddha tradition of alchemy, which was practiced by the rasa siddhas of southern India and the *nath siddhas* of northwestern India during the first millennium AD.

In India, alchemy is called rasavidya, which literally means the "science of mercury," or the "science of the elixir." The word *siddha* means a "perfected one." Unlike the Brahmanical priests of the orthodox Vedic culture, the alchemical siddhas did not view themselves as part of organized Vedic society. As Professor White put it, they transcended the boundaries of social caste and religious affiliation, and formed a "pool of wizards and demigods, supermen and wonder-workers that all south Asians (and Tibetans) could draw on to slake the thirst of their religious imagination" and "were the most syncretistic landmarks on the religious landscape of medieval India."[4]

The siddhas represented embodiments of the tantric approach to spiritual realization: "Total autonomy, omniscience, superhuman powers, bodily immortality, and a virtual identification with godhead—although not at the expense of one's autonomy—are the aims of the Hindu alchemist, just as they are of the great majority of nondualist tantrikas."[5]

The rasavidya texts, which constitute the historical texts of the Indian alchemical tradition, were composed by the siddhas for the siddhas using the same type of symbolic code language that one finds in the Western traditions of alchemy—a language that is sure to lead one astray if one does not already possess knowledge of the process, having been granted that wisdom by the grace of God or by the blessings of a competent master.

The most important of the medieval texts is the *Rasanarva* (Flood of Mercury), dated to the eleventh century. Although the text is anonymous, it was purportedly written by a certain Bhairava, who comes as the twenty-ninth siddha in a list of exponents of the secret knowledge, indicating a long tradition of oral transmission of this wisdom prior to its ever being written.[6]

India is famous for its long-standing oral traditions of wisdom. Even today, there are Vedic pandits who pride themselves on the memorization of huge Vedic texts containing tens of thousands of verses. This was the dominant form of knowledge transmission for thousands of years. It is thus difficult for Western scholars to date the ancient Indian texts, because most were passed down from generation to generation in an oral form and were written down only at a relatively late stage in the tradition, often on banana leaves, which tend to decay rapidly in the tropical heat and humidity. Unlike ancient Western texts, which were often inscribed on clay tablets or walls of stone, and which therefore can be assigned a definitive date, the ancient texts of India were preserved in the hearts and minds of the people long before they were reduced to written form, and thus present a serious dating problem.

Although the rasavidya texts are the earliest written texts of the Indian alchemical tradition, many of the written Vedic texts are dated to the same period, even though it is generally recognized that the oral texts were composed long before.

The most authoritative of the ancient Indian texts is the *Rig Veda,* which served as the original religious canon for the ancient Vedic tradition and to a lesser extent for the Hindu tradition, which evolved out of the Vedic tradition. The actual composition date of the *Rig Veda* is unknown, with estimates ranging from 4000 BCE to 1100 BCE.

In spite of the fact that the later Hindu tradition is dominated by the practice of yoga, meditation, and so on, one finds little if any mention of such practices in the *Rig Veda*. The primary practice outlined in the ancient text, to which an entire book (mandala) is devoted, is that of producing and consuming the soma or amrita rasa—the food and drink of the gods. It thus appears that alchemy was a dominant form of spiritual practice during the earliest periods of Indian culture.

Angiras and the Angirasas

According to Vedic lore, the first to teach the science of immortality (*brahma vidya*) to ordinary human beings on earth was the great sage and seer Angiras—one of the original seven seers (*sapta rishis*) from whom the seven historical families of Vedic seers descended. Angiras is credited as being the "father of all the *riks*"—or the father of all the mantras of the *Rig Veda*.[7] His chief son was called Agni (fire), who was deified as the messenger of the gods and the first ministrant priest.

In the same way that Horus, the chief son of Osiris, became the fountainhead of a long line of mystery teachers, called the shemsu-hor (the descendants of Horus), who predated the historical Egyptian civilization, so also Agni, chief son of Angiras, became the fountainhead of a long line of mystery teachers called the Angirasas (the descendants of Agni), who predated the historical Vedic civilization.

In the same way that Osiris is credited as the first to ascend into the sky to obtain great immortality, so too is Angiras credited as being first to ascend into the sky to obtain great immortality. Just as Horus eventually followed the footsteps of his father Osiris and ascended into the sky, so too did Agni eventually follow the footsteps of his father Angiras and ascend into the sky. The shemsu-hor and angirasas strove to imitate their illustrious ancestors by following the same path. The *Sama Veda* thus tells us:

> *Hence these men have gone up on high and mounted to the heights of heaven: Go forward! Conquer on the path by which Angiras traveled to the skies!*[8]

In both cases, this was a path of immortality and the sojourners on the path were fueled and nourished by the elixir of immortality. Thus Angiras is not only credited as being the first to ascend into the heavens; he is also credited as being the first to teach how to produce and consume the mysterious substance called soma, the food of the gods, which is celebrated in the *Rig Veda* as the amrita rasa—the elixir of immortality.

The Alchemical Interpretation of Soma

Although Indian alchemy is generally believed to have originated during the first millennium AD with the rasavidya tradition, I would suggest that its roots go much deeper into the ancient prehistory of India. The *Rig Veda* and its ancillary texts provide the first references in human history to an elixir of immortality—namely the soma, the food of the gods.

> *Soma is king. Soma is the food of the gods. The gods eat soma.*[9]

Although it is generally believed that soma was derived from a plant yet to be identified, I would offer the alternative suggestion that it was actually derived from mercury. This is consistent with the Western alchemical tradition, in which the philosophic mercury was symbolized by the word *luna* (moon). It turns out that *soma* also means "moon" and the juice of the soma was called *rasa,* a Sanskrit word that also means "mercury," and was specifically used by the alchemical siddhas to indicate the elixir of immortality.

The idea that the Vedic description of soma is actually an alchemical or metallurgical allegory has also been suggested by various Vedic scholars. Dr. S. Kalyanaraman, a Vedic scholar and author of an authoritative dictionary on ancient languages, recently published a book titled *Indian Alchemy: Soma in the Veda,* in which he presents a detailed analysis of the Vedic mantras demonstrating their hidden metallurgical meanings.

Although Kalyanaraman suggests that the purpose of Vedic alchemy was simply to produce "gold" and other precious metals for ornamental and trade purposes, the numerous Vedic hymns that spell out the use of soma as a sacred elixir to be ingested for health, longevity, and spiritual immortality cannot be ignored. In one *Rig Vedic* hymn, the seers thus proclaim:

> I have tasted, as one who knows its secret, the honeyed [soma] drink that inspires and grants freedom, the drink that all, both gods and mortals, seek to obtain, calling it nectar. We have drunk the Soma, we have become immortal; we have gone to the light; we have found the gods. . . . These glorious [soma] drops are my health and salvation: they strengthen my joints as thongs do a cart. May these droplets guard my foot lest it stumble and chase from my body all manner of ills. Far-famed Soma, stretch out our life-spans so that we may live . . . Make me shine brightly like fire produced by friction. Illumine us . . . enter within us for our well being. With hearts inspired may we relish the [soma] juice like treasure inherited from our Fathers! Lengthen our days, King Soma, as the sun causes the shining days to grow longer. . . . It is you, O Soma, who guards our bodies; in each of our limbs you have made your abode. Our weariness and pains are now far removed; the forces of darkness have fled in fear. Soma has surged within us mightily. We have reached our goal! Life is prolonged! The drop that we have drunk has entered our hearts, an immortal inside mortals.[10]

When we cross-reference the Vedic descriptions of soma to the Western alchemical descriptions of the stone, we find a remarkable set of homologies. For example, in the *Rig Veda* those who were responsible for the production of soma were characterized as *kavis*. The word *kavi* is given the following definition:

> gifted with insight, intelligent, knowing, enlightened, wise, sensible, prudent, skillful, cunning; a thinker, intelligent man, man of understanding, leader; a wise man, sage, seer, prophet; a singer, bard, or poet; of the Soma; of the Soma priest; of the *Ribhus*.[11]

The kavis were especially associated with the soma and the fashioning of the hermetically sealed vessels by which the soma was produced. This is indicated by the fact that they were often associated with the Ribhus—mythical beings credited as being the first to fashion the sacred vessel by which Indra, the king of the gods, drank the soma. It is also indicated by the fact that the word *kavi* is closely related to the word *kavacam,* which among other things indicates the armor or clay luting with which the kavis used to seal their soma vessels. We recall that in the West the sealed alchemical vessel was also said to be "hermetically sealed," after the name of the Hermetic alchemists who sealed them. They also used various types of luting.

Kalyanaraman points out that the word *kavi* is also closely related to the word for "metalsmith" or "metallurgist" in languages closely related to Sanskrit. In ancient Persian, for example, the word for a metallurgist was *kaveh;* in Slovenian it was *kovae;* in Croatian, *kavac;* and in Hungarian, *kovacsol.*[12]

The medieval Indian alchemists who wrote the rasavidya texts, dated from the eighth century AD to the eleventh century AD, also often described themselves as kavis—alchemical wizards.[13] Some Ayurvedic healers who inherited the rasayana tradition (the science of making elixirs) from their alchemical predecessors continue to be called *kavirajas* (royal kavis) to this day.[14]

The word *kavi* thus applies not only to those who originally processed the soma during the *Rig Veda* age, but also to the medieval Indian alchemists who were definitely engaged in metallurgical pursuits—as though they were part of the same age-old tradition spanning thousands of years. This supports our contention that Vedic soma has a metallurgical, rather than an herbalogical, basis.

There is other supporting evidence as well. The *Rig Veda* and the ancient Brahmanic texts state that the kavis purchased the raw materials for the soma from the Mujavats. According to Kalyanaraman, the Mujavats were ancient tribes that lived in the mountainous regions of Afghanistan. These are the regions closest to the Indian subcontinent, where there are naturally occurring sources of cinnabar ore (mercury sulfide).[15] It is also known that these regions were once part of the ancient Indus-Sarasvati civilization, now believed to be the historical Vedic civilization.

Cinnabar occurs in the form of deep red or purple ore that appears to grow in the rock of mountains, like the leafless stalks of a plant. According to the *Rig Veda,* the soma stalks were plucked from mountain rock and then crushed with pounding stones, which made a loud noise. In one Vedic hymn the pounding stones are compared to voracious bulls that roar and bellow as they chew "the branch of the purple tree."[16] After being cooked in a vessel, perhaps to separate the sulfur from the mercury, the result was then filtered using a woolen fleece. The filtered streams of juice (rasa) that came out were described as "shining," perhaps because they consisted of lustrous quicksilver.

There is no doubt that gold was also involved in the process of Vedic alchemy, as it was in Western alchemy. Indeed, in addition to mercury, gold was an important ingredient in the production of soma, as Kalyanaraman demonstrates with numerous references. The gold ore too would have been crushed with pounding stones, whose faces are often described as *hari,* a color that can mean either yellow, amber (golden), or red tinted. After crushing the gold ore, the result was rinsed with water and filtered through a woolen fleece.

The use of woolen filters was common in ancient metallurgical practices around the world, for the flecks of gold would stick to the fleece while the water and bits of stone would pass through. This may very well have been the origin of the Greek myth of the "golden fleece," which was associated with the quest for immortality.

It is interesting to note that the Greek writers were often in disagreement about the actual color of the fleece. Some called it the "golden fleece," whereas others called it the "purple fleece,"[17] indicating perhaps its use for purifying both gold ore and purple cinnabar ore. This duality of gold and purple was also applied to the Greek myth of the phoenix, an ancient symbol of rejuvenation and immortality.

Once the ingredients of the soma were purified, they were placed in a vessel to be cooked over a period that could extend for months. Those associated with the preparation of the soma were thus known as the celebrators of the nine-month or ten-month rite.[18] Likewise, the Western alchemists claimed that the preparation of the elixir could take months of continuous cooking—typically nine or ten months.[19]

In the *Rig Veda,* the vessel of the soma was said to be fitted with armor and made strong as a "fortress of metal" so that it would not leak.[20] Likewise, the Hermetic tradition consistently emphasized that the alchemical vessel had to be made strong and sealed airtight so that the metallic vapors would not escape.

As the soma was being prepared, it displayed different colors. When cooked and purified, it was described as the destroyer of the black darkness.[21] Similarly, in the Hermetic tradition, it was said that the "head of the crow," or the phase of dissolution, was eventually overcome when the material became purified and fit for consumption. It then assumed a glorious white color, which was sometimes called the milk of life, or the "virgin's milk."[22] The Western alchemists also compared the white phase of the elixir to milk curdled by rennet.[23] Similarly, in the *Rig Veda* the "white phase" of the process is described as that in which the purified soma becomes enveloped with curds and milk, or when the waters (molten metals) containing the metallic seeds yield bright milk.

> *Then all the gods rejoice in the juice of this powerful (Soma), when it is enveloped with milk and curds.*[24]

The purified Soma has implanted many a seed in those (waters) desirous of conception, which yield bright milk.[25]

In the Western tradition, the additional colors associated with continued purification of the elixir were described as green, citrine (or amber), and finally purple or dark red. These are precisely the same colors (*hari, harita,* and *aruna*), associated with soma throughout the *Rig Veda.*

It is difficult to imagine that these are mere coincidences, especially given the fact that both processes were designed to produce a sacred elixir—the elixir of immortality—which was assigned similar properties in both traditions. It thus appears that we are dealing with an exceedingly ancient alchemical tradition that dates back to the earliest periods of Indian culture.

The rasavidya texts, which surfaced thousands of years later, provide more-detailed information about the alchemical process than the ancient Vedic texts, but both sets of texts appear to be part of the same age-old tradition. Like the alchemical siddhas, the angirasas—the earliest group of Vedic seers—were not part of any organized civilization. They too were "wizards and demigods, supermen and wonder-workers" who roamed the mountains, forests, and plains, like so many Merlins of old, prior to the crystallization of Vedic civilization.

In fact, there is textual evidence to support the notion that even as the historical Vedic civilization developed and orthodox orders of Brahmanical priests became established, the angirasas remained hidden in the forests, beyond the pale of emerging cities and villages, which they eschewed. A similar dichotomy developed in China, where the alchemical masters were viewed as immortals, who eschewed the cities and villages and preferred to live in solitary mountain haunts, where they could practice their art in secrecy and isolation, hidden from the prying eyes of the world. As in the West, the alchemical tradition in the East was largely an underground and highly secretive tradition, which engendered wonder and mystery in the minds of the common people.

The Three *Bindus*

The tantric symbolism that pervades the rasavidya texts appears to be based upon older esoteric traditions that involved the science of soma. In the *Rig Veda,* soma is often addressed as Indu—a word that means both "mind" and a "drop" of nectar. In the later tantric literature, the word *indu* (drop) is transformed into *bindu* (drop).

There are a number of tantric texts that present an esoteric doctrine regarding three bindus (*tri-bindu*), also known as the *kama-kala* (the unit of desire). The three bindus may be interpreted as three different types of soma drops that taken together are capable of fulfilling all desires. The three drops are called the white-drop (*sita-bindu*), the red-drop (*sona-bindu*), and the mixed-drop (*misra-bindu*), indicating a mixture of different colors.[26] The three drops were also known as *bindu, bija,* and *nada,* respectively.

These three drops are identified with Shiva, Shakti, and the relationship between Shiva-Shakti, respectively. Within the tantric system, the three drops are conceived as the tripartite manifestations of the supreme Shakti (goddess), known as Kali (Blackness), who is one of the wives of Shiva (the Absolute) and the goddess of dissolution and destruction.

> That which is the supreme shakti divides itself into three. Such divisions are known as *bindu* (white-drop), *nada* (mixed-drop), and *bija* (red-drop). Bindu is said to be of the nature of Shiva, bija of Shakti, and nada as the mutual relation between the two by those who are learned in the *Agamas* (revealed tantric texts).[27]

Thus, according to the tantric literature, Kali (Blackness) is the cause of the three drops of nectar. The three drops emerge in sequence such that the white-drop comes first, the mixed-drop comes second, and the red-drop comes last. This is consistent with the classical alchemical process in which the black phase (dissolution) gives rise first to the white elixir (white-drop) and then to a variety of different colored elixirs (mixed-drop), culminating in the final red elixir (red-drop).

In the tantric literature, the three drops are compared to the three luminaries: moon, sun, and fire. The moon is identified with the white-drop, the sun with the mixed drop, and the sacred fire (agni) with the red-drop.

The various forms of the elixir were called "drops" because the preferred method of ingesting the elixirs in the Indian tradition involved suspending the powders in a liquid, which could then be drunk. Although soma was sometimes called the food of the gods, it was much more frequently referred to as the drink of the gods.

Mercury, Mica, and Sulfur

The rasavidya texts are extremely esoteric. They never say exactly what they mean in plain language. Everything is written in a symbolic language to hide the truth from the uninitiated. As in the Western alchemical texts, when they say one thing, they actually mean another. Ayurvedic scholars and other would-be alchemists who attempt to derive the secret alchemical process from these texts are thus immediately caught in a snare from which they cannot escape if they take the meaning of the texts literally.

I will argue that there are two distinct alchemical practices encoded in the texts, which may be called the higher and lower knowledge. The higher knowledge involves the production of the true elixir, or rasa, capable of inducing transmutation in metals and transubstantiation in the body. The lower knowledge involves the production of the mercury bhasma, or ash, which may be understood as the "layman's elixir." It also has many wondrous healing and spiritual properties, but it is only a substitute for the true elixir.

The notion that there are two forms of the elixir—one of which is produced from mercury, antimony, and gold over a period of nine to ten months, while the other is produced as the ash of metals over a shorter period of time—may very well be related to the biblical manna, a substance most likely produced from copper in the form of a white ash or powder.

This lower knowledge, which pertains to the production of the ash, or bhasma, is most clearly revealed in the texts, while the higher knowledge is hidden in symbolic language. Thus, depending upon the skill and wisdom of the seeker, both forms of knowledge are simultaneously available—except that the procedures involved in the higher process are never explicitly spelled out. They are kept hidden and only alluded to.

To give an example, take the three principal ingredients for the elixir, which in the rasavidya texts are called mercury (rasa), mica (abhraka), and sulfur (*gandhaka*). These are specifically identified with the sexual seed of Shiva, the sexual seed of Shakti, and the menstrual blood of Shakti, respectively.

Upon reading the texts, anyone uninitiated in the secret tradition would automatically think that mica (an aluminum silicate) and sulfur (a chemical element) were used to process the mercury. Such assumptions now form the basis for the pursuit of the mercury bhasma by vaidyas (Ayurvedic physicians) throughout India even today. But many vaidyas have attempted to replicate the secret formulas throughout the course of their entire lives, using mica and sulfur, with very limited success. They may have succeeded in binding the mercury and even producing a type of mercury bhasma (ash), but in every case the mercury still retains its native nature (and hence some level of toxicity), and never manifests the type of spiritual and transmutative power ascribed to it by the ancient texts. There is a reason for this.

The truth is that mica and sulfur are but code words for something else. In effect, mica and sulfur in the Indian alchemical tradition play the same role that salt and sulfur play in the Western alchemical tradition. According to Philalethes and others, these elements were never used to perform the real, or higher, work. They are symbols for something else.

The primary distinction between the Western and Eastern traditions is that the genders of the sulfur and the mercury are reversed. In the Western tradition, the philosophic mercury was called the "white wife" and the red sulfur was called the "red man." In the Indian tradition, the philosophic mercury was identified with the white semen of Shiva (masculine) and the red sulfur was identified with the red menstrual blood of Shakti (feminine).

In the Western tradition, the red sulfur represents a finely divided form of gold, called "our gold," which is obtained by digesting gold in antimony and mercury during the initial phases of the work. It is well known that both molten antimony and liquid mercury are capable of dissolving gold, like an acid. Moreover, it is known that in its finely divided form, gold assumes a purple and then a deep red color. That is why colloidal gold suspensions have a purple or reddish color. The red powder of gold obtained by this secret method was called red sulfur, because it has the potential to bind or dry up the mercury, just like sulfur.

To start the process, the red sulfur and the philosophic mercury must be married to each other, by being placed together in a sealed vessel and digested over a moderate heat. In the Western tradition, this was called the marriage of the red man to his white wife. The stages that emerge, and which involve the progressive drying up or calcination of the mercurial mixture, display various colors, corresponding to black, white, yellow, and red—all of which may be viewed as forms of the elixir.

In the rasavidya tradition, these various forms of the stone were symbolized by mica, which was assigned the colors black, white, yellow, and red.[28] Mica (a stone) thus serves as the symbol of the actual elixir, or philosopher's stone, in the rasavidya texts.

More specifically, mica signifies the seed of Shakti, which may be understood as the transmuted feminized seed of Shiva (mercury). The feminization of the masculine seed occurs as soon as the seed of Shiva (philosophic mercury) becomes united with the menstrual blood of Shakti (the red sulfur) in the womb or alchemical vessel. In time this spiritual union gives rise to the form of black mica signifying Kali (the phase of dissolution).

It then evolves into the form of white mica signifying the lunar-bindu; then it becomes the yellow mica signifying the solar-bindu; and finally it assumes the form of the red mica, signifying the fiery-bindu. The mica is not an ingredient in the process, nor does it correspond to the mineral of that name. It symbolizes the various phases that the elixir goes through once the seed of Shiva has become united with the menstrual blood of Shakti within the alchemical womb.

This interpretation is consistent with the meaning of the Sanskrit word for mica, *abhraka,* which literally means a "water-bearing cloud" or "water-bearing stone." The water is the mercury, which is bound up in the cloud or stone. It was thus a common metaphor in the *Rig Veda* to compare clouds to mountains, stones, or rocks.

Mica is literally a "stone"—and in the rasavidya tradition it was the symbol for the philosopher's stone. We note that the word *abhra* is also a synonym for gold—hence, abhraka represents the true and exalted form of philosophical gold, the elixir of immortality.

Swooned, Bound, and Killed

In the text called *Rasanarva* (Flood of Mercury), the term *rasa* is given a specific technical meaning. It refers to mercury that has been swooned, bound, and killed.[29] These three transformations constitute the "hump" that the alchemist must overcome before the rasa (elixir) can be obtained. All three aspects fall under the general heading of swooning. A famous verse from the *Rasanarva,* which is repeated in later texts, states:

> *Swooned, rasa, like the breath, drives away diseases, killed it revives itself, bound it affords the power of flight.*[30]

The proper sequence is swooning (*murchana*), binding (*bandhana*), and killing (*marana*). This follows the same sequence described in the yogic texts concerning breath control, or *pranayama,* which employs the same terms.

By repeated alternation of the breath using the left and right nostrils, the two peripheral channels known as the *ida* and *pingala* become awakened and enlivened. When the breath is retained at the end of inhalation or restrained at the end of exhalation, the *prana* (vital energy, inherently controlled by the breath) is forced into the middle channel (*sushumna*), which leads to the third eye. At that point, the two peripheral channels become swooned, or deflated.

In order to prevent the breath from returning to the two peripheral channels, the yogic texts prescribe various bandhanas (locks), which keep the prana energy bound in the middle channel. When the prana becomes bound, it rises up the spine (the middle channel) and ascends to the third eye, which is also known as the "killing" eye of Shiva. It is at this stage that the bound form of individual awareness becomes "killed" and transformed into unbounded universal consciousness. This liberated form of consciousness then ascends into the seventh, or crown, chakra, and blossoms into the thousand-petaled lotus, which drips with the nectar of immortality.

Because of the homologies between the external alchemical work and the internal breath work, the practice of both Indian and Chinese alchemy was often described as a "work in two parts"—one concerning the outer preparation of the elixir and the other concerning the inner preparation of the prana (subtle breath), or chi (subtle energy). To obtain true immortality, one must become the master of both.

When the red sulfur (pingala) and the liquid mercury (ida) become united within the alchemical vessel and subjected to heating (*tapas*), they then become swooned. At this stage, the material exhales an invisible vapor, or "breath," which condenses and is returned to the material below. This process "washes" away the "diseases" of the metal, which correspond to its various veils of ignorance. This is reflected by the statement "swooned, rasa, like the breath, drives away diseases."

Upon being swooned, the moisture of the matter gradually begins to dry up, and as it does so, it emits a dark vapor, which is visible. The drying up of the matter is called "binding." It binds the mercury into fine black particles. When bound, the mercury flies up as a dark vapor composed of fine black particles, which then settle back down and accumulate at the bottom of the vessel as a dry black powder—the ashes of the phoenix. This stage, where the bound mercury flies up as a dark vapor, is reflected by the statement "bound it affords the power of flight."

When the dark vapors cease to arise and the entire material resides in the bottom of the vessel as a dry black powder, the mercury is said to be "killed." This is known as the phase of death and dissolution. The old body of the phoenix has been completely reduced to ashes. But from those ashes a new body is resurrected—as the white form of the elixir, which represents the resurrected body of the phoenix. This stage, where the killed mercury is revived or resurrected, is reflected by the statement "killed it revives itself."

Once the mercurial matter has been swooned, bound, and killed, it is then resurrected as the rasa—the mercurial elixir of the first order. Multiple killings are required to raise the rasa from white, to green, to citrine (yellow), to its final red form. It is then ready to undergo the process of multiplication to increase its quantity and potency. Once multiplied, it can be fermented with gold to create the projection powder, capable of transmuting base metals into gold.

Piercing

The whole purpose of Indian alchemy was to "pierce" the veil of ignorance so that matter could recover its true "spiritual" nature and become capable of reflecting consciousness. In the rasavidya texts, this is called *vedha* (piercing)—a divine act that is fundamental to both the transmutation of the metals (*lohavada*) and the transubstantiation of the body (*dehavada*). This follows the basic principle recorded in the ancient aphorism:

Yatha lohe, tatha dehe
[As in metal, so in the body.[31]]

In the original Indian and Chinese traditions, the emphasis was not upon the transmutation of ordinary metals into gold. What value would that have in the pre-civilized world, where there was little to buy? The primary emphasis was upon the spiritual transformation that resulted from ingesting the elixir. Nevertheless, the transmutation of metals into gold was recognized and used as a test to determine the true power of the elixir. As the *Rasanarva* states:

> Rasa ought to be employed in this way. When it pierces a metal and the body, it behaves in an identical way. First test the rasa on a metal, then use it on the body.[32]

Piercing the metals or piercing the body (and consciousness) involves piercing the veil of ignorance that covers ordinary matter and prohibits the particles of matter from reflecting consciousness. It works in the same way in both the body system and the metals because both the body and the metals are ultimately composed of "veiled" forms of matter, which have latent conscious properties. This means that the true science of alchemy transcends ordinary chemistry and physics—neither of which recognizes the conscious properties of matter.

The seers and siddhas developed the science of alchemy on the basis of their powerful mental vision—which enabled them to literally "see" the subtle currents of conscious energy in their own bodies and in the environment. When the veil of ignorance became pierced and consciousness became awakened in ordinary matter, then the matter was said to become *medhya*—juicy and fit for sacrifice (*medha*). Only then is it fit to be offered into the sacrificial fire for the nourishment of the celestial gods or offered into the fire of digestion for the nourishment of the mind and body. The true elixir of immortality links consciousness and matter, and creates a balance between the two.

The Eighteen Operations of Rasavidya

The rasavidya texts traditionally prescribe a total of eighteen *samskaras* (operations) for the production and use of the mercurial elixir.[33] These eighteen samskaras serve as stumbling blocks for all those who would attempt to replicate the process on the basis of the texts without divine insight or the guidance of a master. The problem is that most scholars and commentators have no understanding of the alchemical process and thus take the eighteen samskaras to be procedural steps of a recipe—which they are not. As a result, the whole science has been completely lost and obscured.

The eighteen samskaras can be divided into four sets: (1) the first eight pertain to the actual production of the elixir; (2) the next four pertain to the processes of multiplication; (3) the next five pertain to the process of projection and the transmutation of the metals; and (4) the last samskara pertains to the transubstantiation of the body.

The names of the eighteen samskaras are themselves mantras (formulas), which reveal all that needs to be known by one well versed in the art and science of alchemy. According to this science, the first thing one should do is prepare the philosophic mercury and the philosophic gold. Even though this process constitutes the whole key to success, it is not described at all by the eighteen samskaras but is generally classified under the heading of Shodhana—preliminary purification.

As in Western alchemy, the preparation of the philosophic mercury and gold was kept as a hidden secret and was never written down in detail. As in the Western alchemical texts, the prescribed operations or samskaras pertain primarily to the stages of the process, once the philosophic mercury and gold have been obtained. A brief overview of the eighteen samskaras is provided below.

I. The Production Samskaras

1. *Svedana*—"sweating." This represents the initial "wet" phase of the material, in which the mercury vapors ascend as a vapor and then condense on the sides of the vessel in droplets that resemble drops of sweat.
2. *Mardana*—"grinding." When a material becomes "ground," it is reduced to a powder. This represents the phase in which the wet material begins to dry up and is gradually reduced to a dry black powder. In Western alchemy this is described as a battle between two dragons, one with wings (the vapor above) and one without wings (the compound below), which grind themselves into dust or ashes.
3. *Murchana*—"swooning." In the context of the eight samskaras, this represents the phase in which the material emits a dark vapor, the liquid dries up, and the entire compound is reduced to black ashes. It thus incorporates the three aspects of swooning, binding, and killing described earlier. In Western alchemy, this is called the regimen of Saturn.
4. *Utthapana*—"resurrection." In this phase, a white crescent first forms around the perimeter of the material and then the entire compound gradually turns snow white, the color of pure milk. In Western alchemy, this is called the regimen of the Moon, when the stone is resurrected from the darkness of death.
5. *Patana*—"causing to fall," "distillation," or "sublimation." When the white stone is subjected to continued heat, it eventually fuses and becomes volatile once again. This is viewed as a "fall" from its previous dry state and may be characterized as a secondary type of distillation, sublimation, or volatilization, which

takes place about midway through the regimen of the Moon. Regarding this phenomenon, Philalethes states:

> Above all things this is most wonderful, that our [white] stone . . . should of his own accord again abase himself [that is, fall down from its previous state], and become again wholly volatile without any laying on of hands. But if you take the white stone out of the vessel, the same being put again into a new vessel, after it is once cold, it can never be brought to a new operation . . . but with a bounteous fire, it may of its own accord melt, and swell, and by the command of God it shall be endued with a spirit, that shall flie aloft, and the stone to flie within it.[34]

6. *Bodhana,* or *Rodhana*—"awakening" or "sprouting." This corresponds to the phase in which the higher power of the white stone begins to awaken as it "sprouts" into a beautiful greenness, resembling the color of tender sprouts that appear in spring with the thawing of the white snow. In Western alchemy, this is called the regimen of Venus, which follows whiteness or the phase of resurrection.
7. *Niyamana*—"restraint." This represents the citrine, yellow, or amber phase, during which the volatility, mobility, and fusibility of the stone are once again restrained and dryness prevails. In Western alchemy, this is called the phase of Mars, which is once again a "dry" phase.[35]
8. *Dipana*—"kindling," or "enflaming." In Western alchemy, this is called the regimen of the Sun, in which the material finally becomes kindled or inflamed with a reddish purple color, indicating the full awakening of the sacred fire within the stone.

The inflaming of the matter completes the production of the stone, which now appears as a fine, sparkling red powder. It can now be removed from the sealed vessel. We thus find that the first eight samskaras are in perfect agreement with the process described in Western alchemy, regarding the production of the elixir.

II. The Multiplication Samskaras

Samskaras 9–12 delineate the process of "multiplication," which serves to increase both the quantity and the potency of the elixir.

9. *Gagana grasa*—"swallowing mica." In addition to being called abhraka (the water-bearing cloud), mica is termed *gagana* (the atmosphere, sky, or firmament), indicating the heavenly virtue of the stone as well as its ability to expand consciousness. Here we are not talking about the ordinary mineral called mica; we are talking about the red "mica" (stone) that has been produced by the previous eight samskaras. Once the red stone has been produced, it must be potentiated through a process of multiplication. This involves measuring out a quantity of the red stone (philosophical mica), introducing it into a new quantity of philosophic mercury, and then decocting or cooking the combination as before in a sealed vessel. Over a period of about one month, the material will go through all of the same courses or changes observed during the first nine months. When the red stone is first introduced into the philosophic mercury, it becomes as if "swallowed" by the mercury. This is called gagana grasa (swallowing mica).
10. *Charana*—"coursing." This signifies the process of coursing through all of the color changes described previously. During the process of multiplication, the material courses through these color changes much more quickly than before, hence the emphasis is upon the "coursing" of the material.
11. *Garbhadruti*—"softening," or "melting in the womb." This signifies the observed difference in the quality or consistency of the material while it is still in the womb (vessel). At the end of the first eight samskaras, the red stone has the consistency of a fine red powder, which is dry. At the end of the process of multiplication, its consistency is different. It does not and will not congeal into a dry red powder. As long as the material in the vessel is

subjected to heat, it will remain in a softened, fused, or molten state. The sign that marks the end of the multiplication process is thus different from the sign that marks the end of the production process. One should look for a fused, soft, molten red elixir within the vessel (womb) and not a dry red powder.

12. *Bahyadruti*—"outer softening, or melting." To make sure that the material is fully potentiated, it should be tested outside of the vessel as well. When cold, it will harden like gum resin. But when it is subjected to a mild heat, such as that produced by the hand, it will soften like wax; and when placed on a heated surface, such as that of a metal spoon held over a candle flame, it will melt and roll up into a round drop (due to its high surface tension). This red-drop is the red-bindu—the very embodiment of Shakti. The ability of the material to soften or melt outside the vessel is denoted by the term *bahyadruti*.

III. The Projection and Transmutation Samskaras

Having described the process of both production and multiplication in aphoristic terms, the samskaras then turn to the processes of projection and transmutation, which were viewed as a test to determine whether the elixir was ready for human use.

13. *Jarana*—"digestion." The fully potentiated elixir obtained at the end of the multiplication process has the ability to "digest" gold. This involves melting a certain quantity of gold in a crucible and then adding some of the elixir to it. The molten gold and the molten elixir will then fuse together. During this fusion the elixir digests the gold and incorporates the gold into its own nature. This is called digestion.
14. *Ranjana*—"tinting," or "coloration." After the process of digestion has taken place within the furnace, the fused mass should be taken out, poured into a mold, and allowed to cool. Upon

breaking open the mold, one should find that a significant quantity of the gold has been tinted or colored by the elixir, forming a red, glasslike substance. The coloration of the gold by the red elixir is called "tinting." The red-gold glass should then be crushed into a fine powder, called the projection powder.

15. *Sarana*—"flowing." In order to use the projection powder for the purpose of transmutation, one should first melt a quantity of lead, or heat a quantity of common mercury, until it begins to fume. Then, wrapping a small quantity of the projection powder in some beeswax, one should cast it upon the molten lead, or heated mercury, at which point it will melt and flow on the surface of the liquid metal like a red oil. This is called *sarana,* or flowing.
16. *Kramana*—"taking hold." In a short while, the red oil will soak into the liquid metal. When this occurs, the molten pool of metal should effervesce, as tiny bubbles of gas are released, giving rise to a slight hissing sound. This signifies the gentle release of alpha particles from the lead or mercury nuclei, whose "binding force" has been relaxed by the powerful field of consciousness that has now "taken hold" of the molten mass. When the consciousness of the elixir takes hold of the metal, the binding forces that hold the nucleus together become softened and there is a release of alpha particles. The ordinary metal atom is now ready to be pierced.
17. *Vedha*—"piercing." When the molten or liquid metal is actually pierced, one should observe both a color change and a change in consistency. According to Helvetius, the material first turns a brilliant green, and then as it cools it changes from green to red and then to the color of shining yellow-gold, which under assay should test as the finest and purest 24-carat gold. Piercing thus results in transmutation of the base metal into gold. The projection powder carries the "archetype" of gold that guides this process, but the process is actually carried out by the consciousness

of the elixir. Just as our physical bodies respond to the consciousness of our mind, so too do the atomic bodies respond to the consciousness of the elixir, which is the "master" of the consciousness of the ordinary metal atoms after they have been pierced and their consciousness unveiled.

IV. The Transubstantiation Samskara

Once one has confirmed the ability of the elixir to transmute the metals, then it can be used to transubstantiate the body. But before one undertakes this final samskara, the rasavidya texts prescribe a course of bodily purification, called Kshetrikarana—"making (oneself master of) the field."[36] This involves special diets, breath exercises, emetics, and other disciplines.

Just as the philosophic mercury and philosophic gold must be purified before one begins the external alchemy, so too must the *dhatus* (tissues) of the body be purified before one begins the internal alchemy. Once this has been accomplished, then the body becomes a fit "womb" into which the elixir may be sown. The result of this impregnation is the growth and development of the immortal spiritual body, called the *vajra-deha,* the "diamond body." The final samskara that denotes the whole process of bodily transubstantiation is called Sharirayoga—"unification of the body."

Sharirayoga is a general "catch-all" term that includes within its scope a variety of different methods by which the elixir can be used to induce mental enlightenment, awaken various supernormal powers, extend the life span, rejuvenate the physical body, and create the immortal spiritual body. Some of these methods are reviewed below.

Ingestion

The simplest method is simply to ingest the elixir. Because the elixir is extremely powerful, one must be careful not to take too much—otherwise the shakti (subtle energy) that awakens in the body will literally burn up the body—resulting in physical death. Supposedly any of the various colorations of the elixir—white, green, yellow, or red—may be ingested with beneficial effects. The exact nature of these effects is unknown.

According to Western and Eastern texts, it appears that a common method was to dissolve a small quantity of the elixir in some warm water, warm ghee (purified butter), or alcohol. A few drops of this tincture taken on a regular basis were supposed to be extremely beneficial, driving away all diseases, uplifting the mind, and extending one's life span. The *Rasanarva* thus describes a "revivifying water" obtained from the elixir.

> It relates that the alchemist who has drunk three measures of this water swoons and then awakens to find himself transformed and possessed of supernatural powers. He is able to "see into the cracks of the earth [to find buried treasure] throughout the seven underworlds; he is invulnerable to the onslaughts of the gods and antigods alike" . . . "he suddenly disappears from [human sight] and becomes lord of the *Vidyadharas* [possessors of wisdom]."[37]

The quantity and the potency of the elixir that can be safely ingested are likely to vary from individual to individual depending upon their physical purity and level of spiritual development. The texts are obscure on this point, and the exact prescription was probably determined by a master. It appears, however, that the effects obtained directly depend upon the amount of elixir ingested. One text states:

> Eating one pala [a measured quantity of the elixir] renders one invulnerable to disease; two palas produce an increase in semen; three palas confer heightened powers; eating four palas cure baldness; with five palas all wrinkles disappear; six palas afford a telegraphic memory; seven palas destroy all defects of vision; eight palas endow one with a bird's eye view [of the Cosmos] and a life span and powers equal to those of Lord Brahma; nine palas make one the equal of all the gods; ten palas make one a second Shiva (Absolute).[38]

The *Gutika* (Rasa Stone)

The rasavidya texts also describe the use of a *gutika*—a rasa stone, or rasa pill—that is held in the mouth for an extended period without swallowing it. This cannot be the same thing as the red elixir, which would soften and dissolve in the mouth, thus penetrating the body. It likely corresponds to the red-gold glass, which was used for the purpose of transmutation. Because the red glass contains digested gold within itself, its melting or softening temperature is bound to be much higher than that of the red elixir. As such, it would be unlikely to "dissolve" in the mouth. It is conceivable that pieces of the red glass were fashioned into pills or small stones that the siddhas held in their mouths. This is consistent with the texts, which describe the effects of different gutikas in terms of their transmutational power. Unbelievable effects were ascribed to the practice of holding such stones in the mouth.

> A gutika capable of transmuting one hundred times its mass of base metals into gold (one hundred vedha), when held in the mouth for one month, yields a life span of 4,320,000 years. One thousand vedha mercury, held in the mouth for two months, permits one to live as long as the sun, moon, and stars. Ten thousand vedha mercury, held in the mouth for three months, yields a lifetime of Indra [king of the gods].[39]

These time spans do not represent the periods of life on earth. They represent the periods of life in the heavens. In the same way that Lord Brahma, the Creator, was viewed as having a life span that corresponds to the light span of the cosmic egg, equal to 311 trillion light-years, the enlightened souls were also viewed as having various life spans, which correspond to the extent of their expanded consciousness.

In this regard, one who possessed the life span of Indra would have an all-pervading consciousness that spans the entire universe. According to the texts, such an all-pervading state of consciousness can be obtained by holding a gutika, capable of transmuting ten thousand times its weight of base metals into gold, for a period of three months.

The Oil Bath

Although the processes of ingesting the elixir and holding the gutika in the mouth were assigned importance, the supreme apotheosis was ascribed to the oil bath, in which the alchemist fills a cauldron with hot oil laden with the mercurial elixir and then climbs into it. As the unctuous elixir penetrates into every pore of his body, the alchemist then swoons and awakens to find that his body has been completely transformed. In the process, the gross material elements (*mahabhutas*) of his body are pierced and transformed into subtle mental elements (*tanmatras*).[40] He then becomes endowed with all sorts of supernatural powers and ascends to sport in the celestial abode of the gods, with a life of countless years.

The Ultimate Goal of the Alchemical Siddha

In general, the process of Sharirayoga involves the total transformation of the individual on all levels—spiritual, mental, and physical—into a godlike cosmic being. The idea that man is created in the image of God is taken to its logical extreme. The elixir seed that is implanted in the womb of the body literally gives birth to a "son of immortality" (*amritasya putra*) that grows up to become like its immortal father. As one text puts it:

> One becomes the creator, destroyer, and enjoyer [of all things], a maker of curses and boons, omniscient, omnipotent, of subtle and immaculate beauty. Such a man acts at will, creates and destroys at will, moves at will, and himself becomes the Universal Form (*vishvarupa*) worshipped by all the gods, including *Brahma, Vishnu,* and *Maheshvara.*[41]

It is thus apparent that the ultimate goal of the alchemical siddha was not to become a maker of gold; his ultimate goal was to know all and become all—to become one with the Supreme Being and an immortal master of Creation.

Chinese Alchemy

The history of Chinese alchemy has been documented by Joseph Needham in his massive work titled *Science and Civilisation in China,* published in forty-two parts in 1970. Needham notes that "the Chinese theory of the metamorphosis of minerals is . . . fully developed by 122 BC, and probably goes back to 350 BC or before."[42] Of particular importance to the Chinese alchemists was cinnabar (mercury sulfide), which can be found in abundance in many places throughout China and which was inextricably linked with the production of gold. One Chinese authority on the subject, Ko Hung (ca. AD 300) wrote:

> When the manuals of the immortals (*hsien ching*) say that the seminal essence of cinnabar gives birth to gold, this is the theory of making gold from cinnabar. That is why gold is generally found beneath cinnabar in the mountains.

Needham points out that the story of the philosopher's stone first makes its appearance in Chinese alchemical texts around AD 20. The *Huai Nan Tzu* (second century BC) mentions black, white, green, yellow, and red mercury,[43] which are precisely the colors associated with the elixir in both Western and Indian alchemy. Antimony was also known in ancient China. Needham thus explains that by the time of the Warring States period (480 to 221 BC), the process of separating gold from silver using antimony was already in practice.[44]

The notion that gold could be artificially produced by alchemical means was also known to the Chinese. For example, an imperial edict issued in 144 BC specifically prohibited the production of gold by alchemical means, on pain of death.[45] It is also clear that the ancient Chinese viewed the science of alchemy as a source of an elixir of immortality.

In 133 BC an alchemist was received by Emperor Wu because he claimed that

> he had discovered the secret of immortality. . . . The alchemist said the Emperor must first worship the goddess of the stove in his own person; this would enable him to invoke spiritual beings who, when they appeared, would render possible the conversion of cinnabar into gold.[46]

As in the West, the procedures of the Chinese alchemists were kept as deep secrets and described using symbolic language. The fundamental principles involved in Chinese or Taoist alchemy are explained in terms of the yin and yang principles, which are represented in external alchemy by lead and mercury, respectively. The "lead" involved may very well be antimony, which was traditionally associated with "lead" in Western alchemy, where it was variously known as "our lead" or the "son of Saturn."

The principles of yin and yang were obtained in the form of "lead" and "mercury" by heating their native ores. These two materials were then placed inside the crucible, consisting of two clay pots, one overturned on top of the other (placed mouth-to-mouth), and then luted so that the vapors could not escape. By so doing, the upper and lower crucibles, which contained the yin and yang principles, were conceived as an image of heaven and earth, and sometimes compared to the cosmic egg.[47]

The sealed crucible was then heated over a bed of coals for an extended period of time. At the end of the prescribed period, the crucible was allowed to cool and then opened. If the operation were successful, the essence of the elixir would have ascended (sublimated) to the upper part of the vessel, where it was collected by a feather and then either added to other substances, placed in the crucible and heated again, or directly ingested. It was to be ingested at dawn, facing the sun.

The goal of Chinese alchemy was the preparation of an elixir usually called *huandan* (Elixir of Return), which was said to grant immortality, illumination, mastery over the elements, and control over gods and spirits. The word *dan* (elixir) also signifies cinnabar, which indicates the importance of mercury in the alchemical process—and also emphasizes the purple-red color of the elixir.

The Philosophy

The underlying philosophy of Chinese alchemy involved the concept of the Tao (the One), which is divided into two principles, yin and yang, which oppose each other in their actions. All of the opposites in the universe can be reduced to these opposing forces.

The Tao is the Absolute Oneness that underlies all duality. Yin and yang represent the polarization of that Oneness in the realm of duality. The principle of yang governs such things as maleness, the sun, creation, heat, light, heaven, and dominance, while the principle of yin governs such things as femaleness, the moon, completion, cold, darkness, material forms, and submission. It is held that the yang principle creates all of the spiritual forms in heaven, while the yin principle creates all material forms on earth. Creation is governed primarily by the principle of yang, which exists above, but the completion of the created thing is governed by the principle of yin, which exists below.

Yin and yang constantly produce each other in a cyclic manner such that no one principle continually dominates or determines the other. All of the opposites such as health and sickness, wealth and poverty, power and submission are due to the temporary dominance of one principle over the other. Since it is impossible for one principle to dominate over the other forever, all conditions are subject to change into their opposites.

Because one principle produces the other, all phenomena also have within them the seeds of their opposite state, even if they are not apparent. Thus sickness contains the seeds of health, health the seeds of sickness, and so on.

The cyclical reversals of yin and yang were believed to govern the process of creation through the agency of the five material agents, *wu hsing* or *wu xing*—wood, fire, earth, metal, and water—which may be understood as fundamental principles that can be applied to all things.

The Taoist schools of thought universally held that the reality of the world consisted of the realm of principles or laws (*li*) and the realm of material force (*ch'i*). The principles were said to govern material force, and material force, in turn, was said to make manifest the principles. The ultimate origin of principle lay in a single principle called the Great Ultimate (Tao ch'i), which emanates from heaven and manifests itself as the two forms of chi (or subtle energy) with the properties of yin and yang.

Within the realm of Taoist alchemy, the yin and yang principles were identified with lead and mercury, and the elixir of immortality represented their transcendental union, which lay beyond all duality. Some schools of Taoist alchemy shifted the symbolic identities such that mercury represented the yin principle, while sulfur represented the yang principle. One should be very careful in assuming that ordinary lead, mercury, or sulfur is indicated here. As in the Western tradition, the words were "code" words within a highly technical esoteric tradition.

The Practice

The predominant form of alchemy practiced in the earliest periods of Chinese culture was known as external alchemy (*weidan*), which involved the production of actual material elixirs designed to be consumed by the aspirants.

Starting around the fourth century AD, the emphasis gradually shifted to the internal practice of alchemy (*neidan*) involving breath work, meditation, and control over the subtle *chi* energies within the body.

Whether the practice involved external or internal alchemy, the student was expected to progress until, as some texts put it, "Heaven spontaneously reveals its secrets."[48] To arrive at this condition of spontaneous revelation, the practice must first proceed under the close supervision of a master, who provides the "oral instructions" (*koujue*) necessary to understand the alchemical processes within oneself.

For the spiritual adepts of the Chinese tradition, the practice of alchemy thus lay at the very heart of their spiritual tradition. It served as the practical aspect of their spiritual science, designed to render the soul immortal and filled with spiritual wisdom.

The fact that the ancient Chinese practice involved the same basic materials and procedures used by Western and Indian alchemists suggests that we are dealing with a very ancient science—a hoary tradition that once permeated the ancient world, originally extending from China in the East to Egypt in the West, and then later to western Europe.

Amazingly, this widespread tradition is largely ignored in conventional theories about human history, even though it arguably formed the heart and soul of the earliest cultures and civilizations on earth. I hope to address the historical implications of this subject in a future volume. My focus here has been upon the substance of the tradition, not upon how it was initially disseminated.

SIX

The Missing Ingredient

The Risks of Public Disclosure

Throughout history, the practitioners of alchemy have done their best to hide their secrets from the general public and even from the secular authorities of the time—probably for good reason. The ancient alchemical sages believed they were under a mandate from God to keep their wisdom secret—and to comply with the will of God, they did so. The knowledge was generally passed down orally along hereditary lines involving initiatory rites and strict oaths of secrecy. Any public revelations of their sacred practice were kept veiled under a thick shroud of symbolism, not to be taken literally.

With the advent of European alchemy, the alchemists came under siege by both secular and religious authorities and were forced underground. Even though they longed for the day when their wisdom could be made public, they still believed that the time decreed by God had not yet come, and that clear public revelation of their knowledge would deserve an *anathema maranatha*—a terrible curse. And so they largely kept secret their practices and their true identities.

Yet in some cases, they became exposed. For example, Philalethes recalls one instance[1] during a general pandemic when out of compassion for those dying around him he went against his better judgment and began to treat the sick with his elixir. The result was that his patients miraculously recovered, almost immediately, while the others died. Within a few days, he was besieged by crowds seeking his help, and his secret was exposed. He had to escape under cover of night using a disguise to preserve his life from those who sought to steal his elixir or any alchemical gold they imagined him to have.

But times have changed, or so I believe. We now stand on the cusp of the Age of Aquarius, when the knowledge of the elixir and the elixir itself are destined to become the province of the common man. As a result, I feel compelled to reveal secrets that have never before been revealed—in clear and unmistakable scientific terms. My friends and colleagues, who fear for my life and tremble at the thought of violating the secrecy that has been maintained for thousands of years, have advised me against this. But against their advice, I am going ahead. Like Prometheus, who gave to mankind the knowledge of fire, I too may be eternally cursed for my deed. But it is a risk that I am willing to take for the potential betterment of mankind.

I am not a naive fool, however. Given the enormous implications of the elixir, which, among other things, has the potential, eventually, to drastically change the economic conditions of modern human society, it would be a serious mistake for me to continue my practical research with the publication of this book and the disclosures contained herein—especially the disclosures to follow. It is one thing to tout the elixir as a panacea for all ills, as a source of an inestimable treasure of gold, and as an elixir of immortality, and it is quite another to actually possess the elixir, demonstrate its power, and promise to distribute it to the needy public. Publishing a formula on how to make gunpowder is quite different from actually possessing tons of gunpowder and promising to distribute it.

This last analogy is not completely inappropriate. In the biblical tradition, the practical and theoretical knowledge about the elixir was symbolized by the Tree of Knowledge. But this was no ordinary tree. It was specifically described as the Tree of the Knowledge of good and evil. The elixir has the potential to do enormous good in the hands of good men and women, but it also has the potential to do enormous evil in the hands of evil men and women. If misused, the elixir can kill you—or drive you insane.

If the elixir is used wisely, for the sake of good, it has the potential to elevate human consciousness beyond anything dreamed of—it has the potential to save the human race and deliver us to the gates of paradise. But if used unwisely, for the sake of evil, it has the potential to destroy the human race and deliver us to the gates of hell.

If you take the alchemists' words at face value, once one knows the materials and procedures involved, the production of the elixir is as easy as baking a cake by following a recipe and could be performed by anyone anywhere. Public revelation of the alchemical secrets is thus like opening Pandora's box. There will be no turning back. The human race will then have to choose whether to step through the gates of heaven or those of hell. Can you see why my friends have advised me against this?

Through years of research, introspection, and study I have stepped up to the precipice and can now clearly see the goal. It is as plain as day. I now have a choice. Should I make the elixir for myself and my friends, while keeping the knowledge secret, or should I reveal the knowledge to the general public for the potential betterment (or destruction) of all mankind? The certain and safe road is the first choice. The uncertain and dangerous road is the second choice. Against the advice of my friends, I have made the second choice. Why?

The answer to this question lies beyond the scope of this book. Suffice it to say that I believe I am acting in accordance with the will of God. As Philalethes put it:

> All Sons of Art . . . write and teach according to that permission which the Creator of all things hath given them.[2]

That permission is not granted by anyone else. It is granted by the will of God, which one must sense within oneself. No matter what rational arguments I might give to justify my choice, the bottom line is that it is an act of faith. I have faith that the time has finally come to reveal the secrets that have been hidden since the beginning of time. I have faith that human society as a whole is ultimately guided by the will of God—and in the end will be delivered to the gates of paradise. We may have to endure some turbulence in the interim, but we will get there. That is my firm conviction. What would you do in my shoes?

Don't get me wrong. I am nothing special. I am but an ordinary person here to deliver an extraordinary message. The message comes from God and what humanity does with the message is up to God. The message concerns the elixir, but it is not the elixir itself. In an ironic twist of fate, the same knowledge that caused Adam and Eve to be expelled from the gates of paradise may very well deliver us back to the gates of paradise. This is the knowledge of good and evil as it pertains to the elixir (or tree) of life. The actual "tree of life" is something else, which can be developed (or grown) on the basis of this knowledge. But I am not its grower, nor can I be. I must renounce all attempts to actually make the elixir in order to deliver the message.

And so, having reached the brink of the precipice, where the goal is clearly in sight, I have had to pull back and discontinue my practical work so that the information herein might be brought to light. Do with it what you will—or what God wills. I can help you no further. With the publication of this book, my job is done. May God help us all.

The Blessed Greenness

There is one piece of information missing from the material presented above, which Philalethes describes as the "Gordian Knot," which "unfolds to a knower of it our secrets."

> We have likewise declared, that the preparation of the true Philosophical Mercury is difficult, the main knot lying in finding

> Diana's Doves [the philosophic mercury], which are folded in the everlasting arms of Venus [the blessed greenness], which no eyes but a true philosopher ever saw. This one skill performs the mastery of theory, enobles a philosopher, and unfolds to the knower of it our secrets. This is the Gordian Knot, which will be a knot forever to a Tyro in the Art, except the Finger of God direct, yea so difficult that there needs to be a particular grace of God, if anyone would obtain the exact knowledge thereof.[3]

A careful reading of the ancient texts suggests that the philosophic mercury is prepared from pure mercury and pure antimony. But if one buys pure mercury and pure antimony from a chemical supply house and then decocts them together in a molten mixture, one will never see the blessed greenness—one will never see the quickening or greening of the mercury—no matter how long the decoction is continued. Therein lies the Gordian Knot that must be unraveled.

Based upon this, some have argued that the term "mercury" itself is a code word for something else, perhaps an acidic liquor obtained from herbs. Philalethes denies this notion and refers to such imitators of the art as "thick skulled and of wretched wit."[4]

> Therefore let the Sons of Learning know that the matter of Common Mercury, ought and can pass into the matter of Philosophick Mercury, although not into the whole Substance which is beheld in it.[5]

In addition to the philosophic mercury, one should expect to obtain another substance, green in color and dry in consistency, that is not itself derived from common mercury. The question is: What is this green substance?

The alchemists referred to it by various names. It was called the royal herb, the green lion, the green toad, the arms of Venus, the vegetable humidity, and the blessed greenness without which nothing can spring.[6] It was compared to an alga on a bog or a pleasant lawn of green grass.

But the alchemists tell us that there is an important feature regarding this "grass." It has the potential to grow "flowers" of orange color if the temperature is too hot. This was called "burning the flowers." Philalethes tells us that if you burn the flowers, then your fire is too hot. This provides another sign that one has obtained the right greenness. If you raise the temperature, then the greenness should start to develop orange discolorations, which can be compared to flowers growing on the green grass. According to tradition, both the green grass and its orange flowers are the product of the "spirit" of antimony, which serves to quicken, or give life, to the mercury. But exactly what is this spirit?

The Spirit of Antimony

The ancients held that the performance of the Star Regulus is essential to obtain the spirit of antimony, which serves to quicken, or green, the mercury. This is our first clue. Purchasing pure antimony from a chemical supply house is not good enough. It will not produce the effect. The antimony has to be produced by means of the Star Regulus.

The Star Regulus involves the use of metallic iron as a catalyst to remove the sulfide from the stibnite, so that pure antimony metal can be obtained. This has led some to suppose that the actual "spirit" of antimony is iron. The presumption is that some particles of metallic iron are carried down by the molten antimony and captured in the regulus below. Thus, when the regulus is mixed with mercury and heated, the iron is carried along as an impurity. But you can take pure antimony and iron in any proportions you want, mix them with mercury, decoct them together in a sealed vessel for as long as you want, and you will never see the blessed greenness. The spirit of antimony is not iron. So what else could it be?

The second clue comes from the fact that the Star Regulus starts with antimony ore—or stibnite, which is found in nature as a blackish mineral deposit. But the alchemists held that not just any stibnite will do. It has to be the right kind of stibnite, which contains more of the mysterious "spirit" than others. For this reason, the alchemists sought out specific stibnite deposits, prized for their spiritous efficacy. What does this imply?

It implies that the spirit of antimony must be present in the native ore, such that it is carried down with the antimony as an impurity in the final regulus. To put things into perspective, one has to remember that in ancient times only seven basic metals were known—copper, silver, gold, mercury, lead, iron, and antimony. The stoichiometric laws of chemistry had not been developed and many chemical elements, including metal elements, had not yet been identified. This was true even at the time of the medieval alchemists. Is it possible that the mysterious spirit of antimony that causes the mercury to ferment or quicken into a blessed greenness was actually a chemical element, unknown at the time, which was recovered along with the molten antimony as an impurity? After numerous failed experiments in my attempts to develop philosophic mercury, this was the hypothesis that I set out to explore.

It is well known that stibnite deposits often occur along with deposits of gold, silver, lead, and bismuth. Gold and silver have relatively high melting temperatures, while lead and bismuth have relatively low melting temperatures—very close to the melting temperature of antimony. It thus seems reasonable to suppose that they might be recovered along with the antimony as impurities during the performance of the Star Regulus.

We recall that the Chinese alchemists viewed mercury and lead as the metallic embodiments of the yin and yang principles. While it is abundantly clear that they were talking about ordinary mercury, obtained from cinnabar, it is not completely clear that they were talking about the chemical element called lead. They may very well have meant bismuth, which in ancient times was often viewed as a form of lead and is found in abundance in China. Today, China exports thousands of tons of bismuth each year to the world community.

In ancient times bismuth was probably viewed as a form of lead because bismuthinite (bismuth sulfide) is often found along with galena (lead sulfide) in natural mineral deposits. During the recovery of lead, bismuth was likely also recovered, such that the result was actually a bismuth-lead alloy. But bismuth (atomic number 83) was not isolated as a distinct chemical element until 1753, when it was first identified by Claude Geoffrey the Younger. Prior to that time, it was viewed just as a "quality" of the lead with which it was alloyed and had no distinct name.

It turns out that the majority of the bismuth product exported by China each year is produced using an old methodology, which is more or less identical to the Star Regulus. This is possible because antimony and bismuth lie in the same column of the periodic table of elements. This means that they have similar chemical properties. Both can form a sulfide mineral. Antimony sulfide is called stibnite and bismuth sulfide is called bismuthinite. Stibnite is a little more blackish in color, while bismuthinite is a little more brownish, but they have similar mineral properties, and to an untrained eye they appear very similar. Moreover, both minerals are often mixed together in the same deposit, such that it is very difficult to distinguish between them.

Not only do antimony and bismuth have similar chemical properties but they also have similar melting points. This means that if the Star Regulus were to be performed using ore obtained from a mixed deposit containing both stibnite and bismuthinite, then both antimony and bismuth would be obtained in the final regulus. Is it possible that bismuth is the impurity that the ancients called the "spirit" of antimony?

You can test this for yourself—just as I did—and you don't have to perform the Star Regulus to do so. Purchase some pure antimony and pure bismuth from a chemical supply house, mix them together in any proportion you like, and melt them together with a quantity of pure mercury in a sealed vessel. Heat the vessel at a moderate temperature, so as to keep the mixture molten without causing excessive vaporization of the mercury, and keep the temperature constant for several days. Within three days you will see the mixture come to life—it will develop a forest green substance that floats on the surface of the molten metal and looks exactly like a living green plant, such as a moss or an alga.

You can try it with different proportions of antimony and bismuth. In each case, the larger the proportion of bismuth, the larger the amount of green substance obtained. If the bismuth is eliminated, no green substance will be obtained at all. If the antimony is eliminated, the green substance is still obtained. It follows that the green substance comes from the bismuth—not from the antimony.

You can also perform another test. Once the green substance has developed, raise the temperature to the point where the mercury begins to vaporize from below, condense on the cold surface of the vessel above, and then fall back down in droplets, resembling rain falling onto green grass. In time the green grass will blossom with orange flowers. The irregular protrusions of the green substance will turn orange, such that they look like orange flowers on a green lawn.

These two tests taken together fulfill the signs prescribed by the ancients and confirm the hypothesis that bismuth is indeed the mysterious "spirit" of antimony. Because the ancients did not know about bismuth, the only way they knew to obtain this spirit was by performing the Star Regulus using stibnite—but it had to be a special stibnite. The stibnite had to be mixed with bismuthinite.

The King, the Queen, and the Priest

Bismuth (atomic number 83) is an interesting chemical element. It is the last stable chemical element in the periodic table; following it are the unstable radioactive elements. To use an analogy, it can be described as the most "mature" of the stable chemical elements—one that embodies all the other elements that come before it.

If you were to progressively strip away electrons, protons, and neutrons from a bismuth atom, any of the preceding chemical elements could be obtained—at least in principle. In other words, it contains all the stable chemical elements within itself in potential form. In this sense, it is unique. It represents the most mature form of stable matter known to man.

In ancient times, maturity was a sign of spiritual wisdom. The ancient societies were largely guided by the old wise ones, who had developed their spiritual powers over the course of long lives and were deemed embodiments of spiritual wisdom. By analogy, bismuth can be compared to the wisest of the stable chemical elements. It embodies the most mature "spirit" of matter, or, more specifically, the most mature "spirit" of the metals.

Given our modern objective paradigm, this may seem a strange way to describe a chemical element. But it would not have been strange to the ancients at all. They invariably viewed the universe and everything in it as alive and endowed with consciousness—including the elements of matter.

But not all forms of matter are equally conscious. The lighter (less mature) elements are less conscious than the heavier (more mature) elements. The heavier elements, such as the metals, were thus assigned more spiritual power than the lighter elements.

Of the stable elements, bismuth (atomic number 83) is the priest. It embodies the most "spiritual" form of elementary consciousness. By comparison, gold (atomic number 80) is the king. It embodies the most "stable" form of elementary consciousness. Mercury (atomic number 81), on the other hand, is the queen. It embodies the most "fluid" form of elementary consciousness. To prepare the queen for her alchemical marriage, she must be anointed by the priest.

The Preparation of Philosophic Mercury

The preparation of philosophic gold requires antimony. No bismuth is required. The preparation of philosophic mercury, on the other hand, requires bismuth. No antimony is required. Nevertheless, the ancients prepared the mercury with an alloy of antimony and bismuth.

The ancient procedure was to melt the alloy along with the mercury until a homogenous molten mixture was obtained. Then the material was cooled and placed in a mortar to be ground with a pestle. Unlike bismuth, which will form an amalgam with the mercury, the antimony will not. By grinding the material, a dry black powder will evolve out of the liquid mercury, which the ancients called the dregs of the black dog. This is the antimony, now separated from the bismuth. It can be washed off with pure water and discarded. This process is repeated until the mercury comes out bright and shining. The results are passed through a woolen filter to remove any hidden remains of the antimony, and then the filtrate is distilled. The bismuth will fly with the mercury, leaving no dregs behind.

This process was to be repeated a certain number of times, depending upon the "spiritous" quality of the original antimony ore. With each repetition, the mercury became more and more infused with the "spirit" of antimony—namely, finely divided particles of bismuth.

Once the matter was deemed filled with spirit, it was placed in a sealed vessel and decocted until the mercury blossomed into greenness. This demonstrated to the ancients that they had indeed obtained a quicksilver, or living silver—the philosophic mercury.

Once the sign of greenness is obtained, the decoction can be stopped and the material allowed to cool. In this case, the greenness will disappear, and the substance floating on top of the mercury will turn gray. Upon removing the material from the vessel, one will discover that the substance on top is a fine, dry, gray powder, which, when heated in the presence of mercury, turns forest green.

If you send this powder out for chemical assay, it will be identified as bismuth oxide. It is of no use. The gray powder should be separated from the mercury by grinding, washing, filtering, and distillation. The metallic bismuth that remains behind in the mercury, and which to the naked eye is indistinguishable from the mercury, is the spirit that makes the mercury philosophic.

But you don't really need to go through this process. You can leave out the antimony. A decoction of pure mercury and pure bismuth will produce the same green or gray powder and the same philosophic mercury. But since the ancients did not have access to pure bismuth, they had to load the mercury with bismuth using the alloy obtained from the regulus.

That is it. That is the secret that has been hidden from the eyes of the world since time immemorial. Ironically, this secret was hidden even from the eyes of the alchemists themselves, who understood the spirit of antimony in principle but did not understand it in practice as bismuth. Like the illusion of a magician, once the trick behind the illusion is known, the whole thing seems trivial. But this particular trick is not trivial. It is the key that unlocks the most potent and mysterious form of matter that has ever been discovered on earth—a form of matter that is capable of producing real magic, namely, the philosopher's stone, or elixir of immortality.

With this revelation, you, the reader, now hold both keys required to produce the miracle. You now know how to make both the philosophic gold and the philosophic mercury, whose alchemical marriage gives birth to the divine child—the elixir of immortality. Just as the birth of the divine child called Jesus Christ gave rise to our modern age, marked by the letters AD, so too will the birth of the divine child called the elixir of immortality give rise to the coming age. This is the age described in the book of Revelation, where death shall be conquered and the streets of Jerusalem will be paved with gold. We are about to witness the greatest transformation in human society that has ever been seen on the face of the earth. Are you ready?

Notes

Introduction. The Ancient Spiritual Science

1. Raphael Patai, "Pseudo-Democritus," *The Jewish Alchemists: A History and Source Book* (Princeton, N.J.: Princeton University Press, 1994), 51.
2. Ge Hong, *Baopu-zi nei pian* (Inner Chapters of the Book of the Master Who Embraces Simplicity), ca. AD 283–343, available at http://catalogue.nla.gov.au.
3. Patai, *The Jewish Alchemists,* 56.
4. *Chandogya Upanishad* 5.10.4.
5. *Rig Veda* 8:48.
6. Philalethes, *Alchemical Works,* S. Merrow Broddle, ed. (Boulder, Colo.: Cinnabar, 1994), 425.
7. Ibid., 156–7.

Chapter 1. The Art and Science of Alchemy

1. Patai, *The Jewish Alchemists,* 56.
2. Ibid., 133.
3. Michael A. Duncan and Dennis H. Rouvray, "Microclusters," *Scientific American* (December 1989), 110–15.
4. Philalethes, *Alchemical Works,* 408.
5. Ibid., 433.
6. "The Three Treatises of Philalethes," part 2, vol. 2, *The Hermetic Museum* (sacred-texts.com/alc/hermmuse/index.htm).
7. *The Secret Book of Artephius* (www.kessinger.net).

8. Philalethes, *Alchemical Works,* 178.
9. Patai, *The Jewish Alchemists,* 78.
10. Ibid., 79.
11. David Gordon White, *The Alchemical Body: Siddha Traditions in Medieval India* (Chicago: University of Chicago Press, 1997), 449.
12. *Rig Veda,* X.62.6.

Chapter 2. European Alchemy

1. Herbert Stanley Redgrove, *Alchemy: Ancient and Modern* (Charlottesville: Electronic Text Center, University of Virginia Library), 12.
2. W. A. Sibly and M. D. Sibly, translators, *The History of the Albigensian Crusade: Peter of les Vaux-de-Cernay's Historia Albigensis* (Woodbridge: Boydell, 1998).
3. Ibid., 400.
4. Redgrove, *Alchemy: Ancient and Modern.*
5. Ibid., section 65.
6. See Philalethes, "An Open Entrance to the Shut Palace of the King," *Alchemical Works.*
7. Arthur Edward Waite, "On the Philosophers' Stone," *Collectanea Chemica* (London: James Elliot and Co., 1893).
8. Philalethes, *Alchemical Works,* 265.

Chapter 3. Jewish Alchemy

1. Patai, *The Jewish Alchemists,* 8.
2. Ibid., 51.
3. Ibid., 18.
4. Genesis 2:10–14.
5. David Rohl, *Legend: The Genesis of Civilisation* (London: Arrow Books, 1999).
6. Genesis 2:12.
7. Arthur Edward Waite, "The Glory of the World," *The Hermetic Museum,* vol. 1 (London: J. Elliot and Co., 1893), 206.
8. Genesis 8:3–6.
9. Walter Scott, editor, translator. *Hermetica* (Cambridge, Mass.: Shambhala Publications, 2001), vol. x, 339. *Teachings of Hermes Trismegistus.* All four volumes originally published in 1924.

10. Ibid., 339–41.
11. Joseph Davidovits, *They Built the Pyramids* (Sainte-Quentin, France: Geopolymer Institute, 2008), ch. 15.
12. Joseph Davidovits, "Are the Pyramids Made Out of Concrete?" published at geopolymer.org.
13. Exodus 19:12–13.
14. Exodus 19:18–19.
15. The Egyptian Book of the Dead, plate 4.
16. Exodus 16:15–16.
17. Exodus 16:13–14.
18. Philip Yam, "The Spectra of Superdeformed Nuclei," *Scientific American* (October 1991), 26.
19. Ibid.
20. Scott, *Hermetica,* 131.
21. Ibid., 166.

Chapter 4. Egyptian Alchemy

1. Patai, "Pseudo-Democritus," *The Jewish Alchemists,* 51.
2. R. A. Schwaller de Lubicz, *The Temple in Man* (Rochester, Vt.: Inner Traditions International, 1977), 106.
3. Scott, *Hermetica,* 341.
4. Philalethes, *Alchemical Works,* 365.
5. *The Book of Alze,* available at members.tripod.com/MoreEsoteric/Alchemy .BookofAlze.htm.
6. Cited in Graham Hancock's *Fingerprints of the Gods* (New York: Crown Publishers, Inc., 1995), 390. Information taken from *New Larousse Encyclopedia of Mythology*, 14–15.
7. E. A. Wallis Budge, *The Mummy* (New York: Wing Books, 1989), 208.
8. R. A. Schwaller de Lubicz, *Sacred Science* (Rochester, Vt.: Inner Traditions International, 1989), 187–88.
9. Graham Hancock, *Heaven's Mirror* (New York: Three Rivers Press, 1999), 111–13.
10. See E. A. Wallis Budge, *Osiris and the Egyptian Resurrection,* vol. 2 (Andover, Mass.: Dover, 1973), 12.
11. Carol Andrews and Ogden Goelet, *The Egyptian Book of the Dead: Theban Recension* (San Francisco: Chronicle Books, 1994), 116.

12. Scene E2, lines 28–32. Original text, illustrated temple wall, and translation available at pantheon.yale.edu/~sokar/index.html.
13. www.ancient-wisdom.co.uk/Ghizaarchitecture.htm#2.11.
14. *The Book of Alze,* available at members.tripod.com/MoreEsoteric/Alchemy.BookofAlze.htm.

Chapter 5. Eastern Alchemy

1. For a summary article on Ge Hong's work, see Evgueni A. Tortchinov, "Science and Magic," in *Baopu-zi nei pian,* from the 8th International Conference on the History of Science in China. Berlin, August 23–27, 1998.
2. Ibid.
3. Ibid.
4. White, *The Alchemical Body,* 80.
5. Ibid., 143.
6. Ibid., 148.
7. See Monier-Williams, *Sanskrit–English Dictionary* (Oxford: Clarendon Press, 1974), 8, 17.
8. *Sama Veda,* 1.5.
9. *Chandogya Upanishad,* V.10.4.
10. *Rig Veda* 8:48.
11. *Sanskrit–English Dictionary,* 264.
12. S. Kalyanaraman, "Rigvedic Soma as a metallurgical allegory; soma, electrum is deified," article posted on the Internet at www.hindunet.org/saraswati/Somaelectrum.htm.
13. White, *The Alchemical Body,* 323.
14. Ibid., 324.
15. Ibid., 449.
16. *Rk Veda,* X.94.3.
17. See *Greek Lyric III Simonides,* Frag *576 (*from *Scholiast on Euripides, Medea)* and *Greek Lyric III Simonides,* Frag *576 (*from *Scholiast on Apollonius of Rhodes).*
18. *Rk Veda,* X.62.6.
19. Philalethes, "An Open Entrance to the Shut Palace of the King," *Alchemical Works,* 420.
20. *Rk Veda,* X. 101.7–8.

21. *Rk Veda,* IX.66.24.
22. Philalethes, *Alchemical Works,* 315.
23. Ibid., 221.
24. *Rig Veda,* IX.14.3.
25. Ibid., IX.19.5.
26. Sir John Woodruff, *The Garland of Letters* (Pondicherry: Ganesh and Co., 1979), 141.
27. Ibid., *Sharada-Tilaka* I.8–9.
28. Ibid., 154.
29. Ibid., 174.
30. Ibid.
31. White, *The Alchemical Body,* 5.
32. Ibid., 188.
33. Ibid., chapter 9.
34. Ibid., 430–31.
35. Ibid., 433.
36. Ibid., 166.
37. Ibid., 326.
38. Ibid., 316.
39. Ibid., 315.
40. Ibid., 150.
41. Ibid., 315.
42. J. Needham, *Science and Civilisation in China,* vol. 3, sec. 25 (Cambridge, U.K.: Cambridge University Press, 2001), 641.
43. Needham, *Science & Civilisation in China,* cited by S. M. Shires, *Mercuric Pyro-Antimonate,* available at www.geocities.com/smshires.geo.
44. Needham, *Science & Civilisation in China,* vol. 5, sec. 33, page 39.
45. N. Powell, *Alchemy, the Ancient Science* (Garden City, N.Y.: Doubleday and Co., 1976), 31.
46. Ibid., 32.
47. Nathan Sivin, "The Theoretical Background of Elixir Alchemy," in Needham, *Science & Civilisation in China,* 292–97.
48. Cited by Fabrizio Pregadio, "A Short Introduction to Chinese Alchemy," 1996, available at helios.unive.it/~dsao/pregadio/.

Chapter 6. The Missing Ingredient

1. Philalethes, *Alchemical Works,* 400–401.
2. Ibid., 156–57.
3. Ibid., 408.
4. Ibid., 480.
5. Ibid.
6. Ibid., 355.

Selected Bibliography

Andrews, Carol, and Ogden Goelet. *The Egyptian Book of the Dead: Theban Recension.* San Francisco: Chronicle Books, 1994.

———. *Osiris and the Egyptian Resurrection.* Andover, Mass.: Dover, 1973.

Chandogya Upanishad, cited in *Sarasvati River,* by Dr. S. Kalyanraman. Chennai, India: Sarasvati Sindhu Research Centre, 1997.

The Egyptian Book of the Dead. San Francisco: Theban Recension, Chronicle Books, 1994, p.116.

Ge Hong, *Baopu zi neipian,* AD 283–343. Available at http://catalogue.nla.gov.au.

Hancock, Graham. *Fingerprints of the Gods.* New York: Crown Publishers, 1995.

———. *Heaven's Mirror.* New York: Three Rivers Press, 1999.

Monier-Williams Sanskrit–English Dictionary. Oxford: Clarendon Press, 1974.

Needham, J. *Science and Civilisation in China.* Cambridge, U.K.: Cambridge University Press, 2001.

Patai, Raphael. *The Jewish Alchemist.* Princeton, N.J.: Princeton University Press, 1994.

Philalethes. *Alchemical Works,* S. Merrow Broddle, ed. Boulder, Colo.: Cinnabar, 1994.

Powell, N. *Alchemy, the Ancient Science.* Garden City, N.Y. Doubleday and Co., 1976.

Redgrove, Herbert Stanley. *Alchemy: Ancient and Modern.* Charlottesville: Electronic Text Center, University of Virginia Library.

Rig Veda: Rig-Veda Sanhita, translated by H. H. Wilson. London: N. Trubner and Co., 1866.

Rohl, David. *Legend: The Genesis of Civilisation.* London: Arrow Books, 1999.

Sama Veda: Hymns of the Sama Veda, translated by Ralph T. Griffin. Livingston, N.J.: Orient Book Distributors, June, 1980.

Schwaller de Lubicz, R. A. *Sacred Science.* Rochester, Vt.: Inner Traditions International, 1989.

———. *The Temple in Man.* Rochester, Vt.: Inner Traditions International, 1977.

Scott, Walter, ed., trans. *Hermetica.* Cambridge, Mass.: Shambhala Publications, 2001.

Sibly, W. A., et al. *The History of the Albigensian Crusade: Peter les Vaux-de-Cernay's Historia Albigensis.* Woodbridge: Boydell, 1998.

Waite, Arthur Edward. "The Glory of the World," *The Hermetic Museum,* vol. I, London: James Elliot and Co. 1893.

———. "On the Philosopher's Stone." *Collectanea Chemica.* London: James Elliot and Co., 1893.

Wallis, Budge, E. A. *The Mummy.* New York: Wing Books, 1989.

White, David Gordon. *The Alchemical Body: Siddha Traditions in Medieval India.* Chicago: University of Chicago Press, 1997.

Woodruff, Sir John. *The Garland of Letters.* Pondicherry: Ganesh and Co., 1979.

Index

Books of Related Interest

Creating the Soul Body
The Sacred Science of Immortality
by Robert E. Cox

Spagyrics
The Alchemical Preparation of Medicinal Essences,
Tinctures, and Elixirs
by Manfred M. Junius

Fulcanelli and the Alchemical Revival
The Man Behind the Mystery of the Cathedrals
by Geneviève Dubois

The Morning of the Magicians
Secret Societies, Conspiracies, and Vanished Civilizations
by Louis Pauwels and Jacques Bergier

The Mysteries of the Great Cross of Hendaye
Alchemy and the End of Time
by Jay Weidner and Vincent Bridges

Alchemical Healing
A Guide to Spiritual, Physical, and Transformational Medicine
by Nicki Scully

The Magus of Freemasonry
The Mysterious Life of Elias Ashmole—Scientist, Alchemist,
and Founder of the Royal Society
by Tobias Churton

Isaac Newton's Freemasonry
The Alchemy of Science and Mysticism
by Alain Bauer

INNER TRADITIONS • BEAR & COMPANY
P.O. Box 388, Rochester, VT 05767
1-800-246-8648
www.InnerTraditions.com
Or contact your local bookseller